The Makings Of Queen

J.A. BUTLER

Contents

Acknowledgments

This book is dedicated to every woman who has ever found themselves in an abusive relationship, especially at a young age. Remember, you all are Queens. Never let any man tell you otherwise. You do not need a king to be a Queen. And a man who puts his hands on you does not love you and is most definitely not a King. Keep your head up, Queens. The right one is out there looking for you.

I also want to give special thanks to Jasmine Shepard, who helped me with some of Brielle's dialogue. Thank you, girl.

Published by DreamWakeWork Publications ©2022

WARNING!

This book is the Sequel to the Best-selling series "Queen" and "Queen: Logan's Story" Books are best if read in Order. ENJOY!

QUEEN 2
Logan's Story

J.A. BUTLER

Prologue

It was the night of my 15th birthday. I was sitting on the edge of my parents' bed playing with my new DS they had just gotten me. My parents were getting ready to go out. As much as I didn't want them to go, they were not trying to hear it.

"Please, mom. It's my birthday, and you guys are just gonna leave me here? Like that's just rude." I pouted and turned my game off. Mom was sitting at her vanity putting on some earrings, and dad was in the closet still trying to pick out a tie.

"Queen, as much as you complain about us treating you like a baby, you sure are acting like one," my mother said, looking at me through the mirror. I didn't care that my parents were going out. It was just because I knew what them going out meant. My uncle would be here to *watch* me. As old as I was, they still didn't trust me in the house by myself.

"Queen, stop with the whining. You know how I feel about that," my dad said, giving me a stern look as he exited the closet. My parents were strict, and my dad was a firm believer of physical discipline. My dad's way of thinking was still back in the sixteen hundreds. Women were supposed to obey, and children should not speak unless spoken to. As you can imagine, I was punished a lot. I was very opinionated about a lot of things and my dad did not like that one bit. I pleaded with my mother some more and stopped when my father gave me the *"this is your last warning"* look. As I watched them finish getting ready, there was a knock at the door. The hairs on the back of my neck stood up just at the thought of who was on the other side.

"Queen, go open the door; it should be your uncle," my father said with much authority in his voice. Because I was already pushing my limit for the day, I did it without giving him any lip. But I mumbled under my breath the entire way downstairs. With much hesitation, I opened the door to see my uncle Deon standing there. He was smiling and holding a pink glittery gift bag. I assumed it was for me.

"Happy Birthday, sweetheart!" He said as he pulled me into a hug. I tried my best to pull away, but he held me tighter. "We're gonna have *lots* of fun tonight," He said into my ear. I pushed him away from me. He smiled at me as I got out of his way so he could enter the house.

"Deon, thanks for keeping an eye on Queen for us." I turned around and saw my mother coming down the stairs.

"It's no problem, Angelica. You know I love spending time with my favorite niece, especially on her birthday," he said as he handed me the gift bag.

"Thank you, uncle Deon." I took the bag even though I didn't want to. I wanted to beg my mother not to go, but soon as I was gaining the courage to do so, my father descended down the stairs.

"Deon, I was just about to call you," my dad said.

"No need, my brother. I'm already here. What, you thought I was gonna flake out on my niece?" Uncle Deon laughed. "You know we enjoy the time we spend together." He winked at me. I didn't understand how my parents were missing all this.

"Well, we don't want to be late for our reservations. So we'll leave you guys to it." My dad said as he grabbed his and my mom's coat. I sat on the stairs, both of my hands trembling from fear. My parents kissed me on the head and told me goodnight before leaving the house. If only they knew this night would change me forever.

A couple hours had passed, and Uncle Deon didn't really bother me. I was grateful for that. After my parents left, he went into the living room to watch tv, and I was in my room still playing my DS. I was filled with so much fear of what was to come. I kept thinking I heard him coming up the stairs, but it was just my ears playing tricks on me. Hours went by, and still, he left me alone. I was grateful for it. It was starting to get late, so I turned off my DS and got ready for bed. I was dozing off when the light from the hallway caught my attention. My back was facing the door and I could see the light on my wall.

"Queen, are you awake?" I heard my uncle Deon ask. I laid there still as a statue. I had to slow my breathing just to make sure he thought I was asleep. He closed the door behind him. I only knew because the light disappeared on the wall. The weight of his body on top of me was suffocating. His musky scent mixed with the stench of alcohol was noisome. He used his hand to cover my mouth as he violated my body. Once he was finished, he kissed me on my forehead and told me happy birthday again. Like I was happy he used my body as his personal playground. I waited until I heard him go back downstairs before I ran to the bathroom to take a shower.

No matter how much I scrubbed, I could still smell him on me. It was useless. I sat in the shower for another fifteen minutes, just crying. Once I ran out of tears, I washed up and went back to my room. I threw on a t-shirt and some sweatpants and got into bed. I had no one to talk about what happened to me. As I laid in bed, I caught a glimpse of the pink glitter gift bag my uncle gave me. I never opened it. Curious, I got up and decided to see what this sick man purchased for my birthday. I sat on the floor and grabbed the bag. I pulled out the tissue paper and there was a box sitting at the bottom of the bag. I pulled it out to discover it was the Sanyo Innuendo prepaid phone from Boost mobile. As much as this man hurt me, I was mad at myself for being excited about the phone. There was also a zebra skin diamante case cover. I hurried and put the case on the phone and got back in bed to set it all up. I stumbled across one of the pre-installed apps. It was called AirG, and seemed to be a chat room of some sort. Bored with nothing else better to do, I made a profile. I took a quick picture for my profile pic, and I was set. Few people hit me up, but they were looking for hookups and asking me to send them nudes. So I wasn't too interested in talking to them. Just when I was about to go to bed, I got a message from a guy named Ness.

Ness: Good evening, beautiful. What are you doing up this late?

Queen: Just laying in bed trying to forget today. Some birthday.

Ness: It's your birthday? Happy birthday hun. How old are you?

Queen: ... I turned 15 today.

Ness: Little young to be on here, don't you think?

Queen: I was just looking for someone to talk to, is all.

Ness: Well, I'm a good listener. What's going on?

I spilled my heart out to a complete stranger. I told Ness everything. How my uncle was touching me for years. How I was scared to tell my parents or anyone else cause I didn't think they would believe me. Ness didn't make it seem like it was my fault. He actually believed me. It felt nice to finally tell someone what was going on. Ness told me the next time my uncle tries to touch me to kick him in his balls as hard as I could. And if that didn't work, to push my nails in his eyes as far back as I could get them. It made me laugh a little. We stayed up until six in the morning talking. Ness lived in New York, had his own apartment, and he had a cat. I told him about my home life and how strict my parents were. We learned a lot about each other. I finally felt like I had someone I could trust.

Chapter One
ONE YEAR LATER

I t's been one years since Ness and I got together. We have talked every day since my fifteenth birthday. Ness drove down to see me a few times and we would get a hotel room for the weekend. I always just told my parents that I was staying over at a friend's house. But this time I was going to see him. I had to think of something creative. The drama club was going to New York this weekend to see some show on Broadway. So, for the last two months, guess who was a part of the drama club? You guessed correctly if you thought of yours truly. I had the permission slip and everything. I didn't even turn the damn thing in. It was all just a ruse for my parents to think I was going with the school. I was overly excited. I just had to make sure I met up with the school group at some point to take some pictures with the group to make it believable. Thankfully my friend Alexa was really in the drama club to keep me updated on their whereabouts. So I was packing my bags to "spend the night" over at Alexa's. She had a car, so she was coming to pick me up to drop me off at the train station so I could be on my way to see my baby tonight.

I was just about done packing when Ness called me.

"Hey, baby. Make sure you're at the station by seven. I don't want you to miss your train." I giggled, "Babe, I'm not gonna miss my train. I promise you that. Alexa should be on her way to pick me up now. I'm just about done packing."

"I know, babe. I'm just really excited to see you. For once you're coming to see me."

"With all the trouble I had to go through to do this, you better be fucking grateful." I laughed as I packed the last little bit of stuff in my suitcase.

"You know damn well I'm gonna make it up to you, girl." I smiled, knowing he would. Ness has done so much for me over the year. After we had been talking for six months, he had me make a P.O. box just so he could send me things and my parents wouldn't find out. He was the sweetest. After everything that happened with my uncle, I was glad to have someone who actually cared about me and my well-being.

"I know, babe, but let me hop off this phone. It's not safe for me to be talking at the moment. I'll text you when I get to the station."

"Ok, baby. I'll be waiting for you when you get here. I love you."

"I love you too." Soon as we hung up, Alexa texted me telling me she was out front. I grabbed my things in a haste and made my way downstairs. I was just about to head out the door when my father called out to me.

"Queen, before you go, your mother and I want to speak with you." I rolled my eyes before I turned around and faced my parents. Of course they wanted to talk to me when I'm pressed for time.

"Ok, I don't have long, Alexa is out front waiting for me," I said, sitting my bag down next to the door.

"What's the rush? You're only going to her house for the night. It'll still be there no matter when you arrive," my mother said, eyeing me.

"I know; I'm just excited." Which wasn't a lie. I was just excited to be able to spend time with my boyfriend and not worry about if someone who knows my parents sees us or not.

"We just wanted to tell you to be safe and enjoy it. It's a wonderful experience for you." My parents went on for about five minutes about how I needed to be safe and be grateful for this opportunity. I was getting antsy. I didn't want to miss my train.

"Mom, Dad, I gotta get going. Alexa has been waiting for a while now," I said, picking my bags up.

"Just remember to call us when you get to New York, ok?" I nodded and headed out the door. I practically ran to Alexa's car. I wasted five minutes talking to my parents, and now we had to rush to the train station.

"Girl, what took you so long? You know we gotta get you to the train," Alexa said as I got into the car.

"Trust me I know. Ness would kill me if I missed this train. But you know how my people are," I said, rolling my eyes.

"Well, forget about them, and let's get your ass to your man, gurl."

"You don't have to tell me twice."

The whole way to the train station Alexa and I talked about all the things we wanted to do while in the Big Apple. Alexa was more excited to go shopping in SoHo. I wasn't worried about the shopping aspect. I already knew Ness probably had bags waiting for me from some fancy little boutique and all the name brands that I love. Most of our weekend was already planned out. First night go see "A Raisin In The Sun" on Broadway *with* the drama club. Afterwards Ness was gonna take me to some party his friend was throwing. Sightseeing was of course part of the plan. There was so much we had to do in two days.

Alexa pulled up to the train station and we said our goodbyes. Well, that is until we see each other later tomorrow. I gathered my bags and made my way into Queen street station. After I got directions to the proper gate and got settled on the train, I texted Ness to let him know I made it and was in my seat. In a few hours, I would be in the arms of my man.

Chapter 2

NESS

I t was almost three in the morning and I was clapping cheeks. Just with some random hoe that slid through the homie's crib. I was just about to bust my nut when Queen texted me.

Queen: I'm three stops away. Can't wait to see you.

I put my phone down and started drilling into shawty. Don't get me wrong, I have mad feelings for Queen. She was very mature to be only fifteen. But we lived in two different states and a nigga had needs. Queen was also easier to manipulate than the women my age. I didn't have to worry about no stupid ass arguments or nothing. I've been grooming her to be the perfect woman. Who said you couldn't build a perfect bitch?

I busted my load all over shawty's ass and cleaned myself up. I didn't have time to run home and shower. So I had to go as is. It was a good thing I kept a bottle of cologne in the whip. When I got in the car, I texted Queen back to let her know I was on my way. I was excited to see shawty for real. It's been a hot minute since I laid eyes on her. I just couldn't wait 'til she was legal so she could officially come down here and stay with me. All this creeping around shit was for the birds. I was too grown to be doing all this. But if this is what it took to get the perfect, obedient woman, then so be it. I had invested a year in lil' shawty, what was two more? I wasn't trying to have another nigga on the bitch I trained. That's exactly what females were, bitches. Dogs you have to train to be loyal and know who their master is. That's why I was glad to find Queen at such a young age. Her mind was still innocent. Her uncle had started that shit, which was fucked up on a lot of levels cause she was so young when he physically touched her. I wasn't about touching and sleeping with children, but now she was much older, he had left room for me to work on her mind. There was still room to manipulate and corrupt her as I saw fit. Which is what I did and was still doing.

It didn't take me too long to reach the train station. I still had some time to spare before Queen's train even pulled in. I wanted to roll up, but I didn't feel like going down the block and risk losing my parking spot. So I chilled in the car until Queen told me she was one stop away. I made sure I had everything I needed before getting out of my car and locking the doors. Walking in to meet her, I was almost knocked over by people rushing to get to their trains. A fool had one time to step on my kicks before I laid their ass out. I got to the exit gate, where Queen should have been coming from. I texted her back to let her know I was here waiting for her. I had the crib already set up for her arrival. I went shopping for her earlier during the day. My living room was filled with bags from Victoria's Secret, Bath and Body Works, Forever 21, etc. I wasn't dropping bands on the high class shit for her just yet. Queen was still young. She had no business walking around in Louis Vuitton, Gucci, and whatnot. At least not yet, she didn't.

It didn't take me long to spot my lil' shawty. Especially since she was hauling ass straight towards me yelling my name.

"Babeee! I missed you," she said, wrapping her arms around me. I returned the hug.

"I missed you too, baby girl. I'm happy you finally decided to visit a nigga," I teased her. I knew how her parents were, so I know she had to go through a lot just to be here.

"Don't start with that bull. Just be glad I'm finally here," Queen argued as she pulled away from me. I grabbed her luggage, and with my free hand, I pulled her by the waist closer to me.

"Are you ready to head out? I know you probably mad tired from that long ass ride." Queen nodded her head.

"Shit, I hope you gonna get me some food cause I'm starving like Marvin, and I don't even know bul." She laughed.

"You think I would have you come all the way out here for a weekend and not feed you?" I asked her. I knew she was only joking. Thankfully I had one of the shorties I fucked around with make dinner earlier that day, so all I had to do was heat it up.

The whole ride back to the crib Queen was giving me the rundown on how the weekend needed to go. It was blowing me. All I wanted to do was chill with her, not be her chauffeur and babysitter. I just nodded and gave the occasional "ok" so she didn't know my mind was absent. I didn't want to fight with her on the first night she was here. But this school trip was getting in the way of everything I had planned.

When we finally got in the crib, Queen instantly ran over towards the couch. It was covered with shopping bags. I had run out of room on the couch that some were on the floor in front of it.

"Is all this for me?" Queen asked, looking back at me.

"Naw, it's for my side jawn," I replied, being a smart ass. Queen rolled her eyes at me and started to rummage through some of the bags.

"I'm going to take a shower, I just know dinner will be here when I get out?" she said as less of a question and more of a playful demand as she smiled. I nodded, taking my jacket off and placing her luggage near the bedroom door. Queen walked up to me and kissed me before heading to the bathroom.

"Thank you, baby. I honestly wasn't expecting all this," she said before disappearing into the bathroom. That was a damn lie. Queen knew damn well I always went out of my way to spoil her ass. I did it cause if she couldn't get it from me, she would find it elsewhere, and I'd be damned if she ever asked another nigga for shit while I was her man. That shit was dead on God. Wasn't nobody sliding in on what I had been building.

I walked into the kitchen to start heating up the food. Ole girl had made flank steak with lobster mac and cheese and white rice. I had to break her off some pipe cause she really threw it down in the kitchen. Always made sure a nigga had a homemade meal.

As the food was heating up, I started setting the table. I was a hood nigga, but bitches always fall for that romantic bullshit. I had the candles with the crystal candle holders. I dimmed the lights and put on some smooth jazz. When did you ever know a nigga in the streets to listen to smooth jazz? My point exactly. I treated Queen just as her name suggests, well at least like a Princess anyway. She had a while to go to get to Queen status. I would continue to do that until she gave me a reason not to.

While I was waiting for baby girl to finish up in the bathroom, I rolled up a fat blunt and just chilled. I let the weed and the jazz do their thing. When I put the blunt out and went to get the food set up, there was a knock at the door. I wasn't expecting anyone for the whole weekend, so I was curious who would be popping up at my crib this late. I opened the door, and to my surprise it was Brooklyn.

She wore a tan trench coat and some red bottom heels, like the bitches be doing in the movies and shit.

"Hey baby, missed me?" She asked, as she squeezed past me.

"Brook, what the hell you doing here?" I asked her as I shut the door. I looked over to the bathroom, and the door was still closed. I walked over to see if I could hear the shower, and thankfully it was still running.

"You did all this for me? Ness, you shouldn't have," Brook said, peeking into the shopping bags that I had gotten for Queen. I needed to figure out how to get her out of here and fast before Queen got out of the shower. Brooklyn was the shorty who so graciously prepared the meal Queen and I was getting ready to enjoy, not that Queen needed to know that.

"Brook, you can't be here right now. Like, you have to go," I said, trying to keep my voice down so Queen wouldn't hear me.

"The fuck you mean I gotta go? If you didn't do all this for me, who the fuck is it for?" Brooklyn was screaming at this point. "I know you didn't have my ass up in here cooking for some bitch." I was across the room in a hot minute choking her ass up. Brook always knew I was in a relationship, so for her to be acting so surprised was wild. Like yea, I knew homegirl wanted to be with me, and I strung her along and shit, but I was always straight up with her. She knew it was never gonna happen. Yet she still tried to ease her way into my heart. But she always failed.

"First of all, don't be disrespectful up in my shit. Secondly, you already knew what it was, so don't play dumb with me. Now take ya pathetic ass home. I'll hit you up once you got your mind right and remember your position on this team," I said, finally releasing her.

"I'm sorry, baby. I know... I just thought-"

"You thought the fuck wrong," I said, interrupting her.

"Who the fuck is this? And why is she calling you baby?" I heard Queen say. Damn, so much for my dirty little secret.

Chapter 3

QUEEN

I couldn't believe I was actually in Ness's apartment. Everything felt surreal, like I was dreaming. This man went on a whole shopping spree before I got here. I turned the shower on and texted Alexa that I made it safely. I will be seeing her sometime tomorrow anyway. As I undressed, I heard some muffled music. I laughed to myself thinking about what Ness could possibly be doing on the other side of the door. I turned my own music on and the sounds of Trey Songz filled the bathroom, as well as the sound of the shower drowning out the rest of the world for just a few minutes. I didn't have much to do since I shaved the night before. I just wanted to freshen up a bit for tonight's festivities.

Ness was my first love; in fact, he was my first everything. I was glad I decided to lose my virginity to him. Obviously, I was not a virgin, considering how my uncle defiled my body more than once. But Ness explained that really, I was because I was so young and couldn't consent to that foul as shit. Ness was the first and only man I ever made love to. Believe me, it was much more enjoyable, and you couldn't tell me that this man didn't take a hold of my v-card.

I had left my luggage with Ness, so I didn't have anything of mine in the bathroom. I looked around to see if I could find anything I could use to wash myself. I looked in the linen closet and found some (what I was hoping were clean) towels and wash rags. I stripped out my clothes and played some of my favorite Trey Songz to help me get in the mood.

"I know you didn't have my ass up in here cooking for some bitch." I was just stepping out of the shower when I heard a female yelling. I was hoping my ears were deceiving me. Ness for damn sure did not have another woman in here while I was here. I hurried and draped the towel around my body, damn near running out that bathroom.

Ness had his back facing me, and was standing in front of a woman who had tan skin and long black curly hair. I wasn't a hater. Homegirl was cute or whatever. I just wanted to know why she was here.

He was telling her that she had to go and had the wrong idea about something. I snapped out of my thoughts quickly when I heard her call MY MAN, baby.

That's when I stepped in with the questions, my arms folded across my chest. They were there to keep the towel in place, but it also added a little extra attitude to what I was saying. His head turned so fast I thought he was gonna have whiplash.

"Queen, go back in the bathroom or the bedroom. I don't really care which, let me handle this," Ness ordered me. I couldn't help but laugh. Cause if he had handled it correctly, my ass wouldn't be out here trying to figure out who the fuck was ruining my weekend.

"There's really nothing to handle just tell me who the fuck she is. Unless you're hiding something," I said with a smirk. I swore up and down I had him where I wanted him. Although I had never been in a situation like this before, Love and Hip Hop had prepared me for this moment. Only thing I was missing was a drink in hand. Them bitches loved to throw drinks.

"Oh, I see now. You playing around with little girls who *think* they grown." I know this woman was not trying to come for me. She needed a reality check cause she was two snaps and a Fruit Loop away from getting her ass beat.

"Honey, you might want to stop right there cause this *little girl* will lay you out on your fake ass." I moved closer to where she was standing, but Ness stopped me.

"Are you protecting this bitch? Trying to be captain save a hoe now?" I said, pushing Ness's head with one hand and holding up my towel with the other.

"Queen, if I have to tell you again, we're gonna have a problem," Ness warned me through clenched teeth. I looked around trying to figure out who the hell was he talking to. Cause he sure as hell was not talking to me.

"We already have a damn problem. Obviously, you can't keep your groupies in check. Had me come all the way out here just to find out you cheating. I caught you red hand-" before I could finish my sentence, my vision blurred, and the right side of my face was stinging. I was in shock. Did this nigga just put his hands on me?

"Stop with all that talking back and take ya ass into the room now!" Ness yelled. I was still trying to wrap my head around what just happened. My eyes burned, threatening to let tears escape. I wasn't going to give this hoe the satisfaction of seeing me cry. So I grabbed my suitcase and went to the bedroom. I slammed the door so hard it rattled on its hinges. After a year of sneaking around and being together, Ness has not once ever put his hands on me. He made it seem like he was against putting his hands on women. All the times I told him about my father doing the same to me, he would threaten to come to my house and beat the living daylights out of him. I would always have to talk him out of it. So how could he do this to me? I could hear them mumbling back and forth for a while.

It made my blood boil to know Ness was out there with some random floozy, and I was in here. He was treating me like a child.

I must have dozed off at some point. I was startled awake by Ness shaking me to get up. I hurried and pulled away from him.

"So what, you're scared of me now? Over a little slap to the face? Be grateful that's all it was. You were being disrespectful. I had to put you in your place. Now come eat before the food gets cold," Ness said everything so calmly. Like it was normal. I didn't want to anger him further.

So I just nodded. Thinking back to earlier, maybe Ness was right. I should have just let him handle it from the start. So much for trying to act like the cast from Love and Hip Hop. I guess things work differently in the real world. We never see what goes on when the camera isn't rolling. Who's to say the females don't get smacked up by their lovers.

Chapter 4

NESS

I wasn't sure what was up with this little attitude change Queen was going through. I never had to tell her to do something more than once. Must be the reality tv shows she be watching. I keep telling her ass most of the shit is scripted. Dinner was quiet. She didn't say much of anything as we ate. I thought about how I could make it up to her. But I needed her to know when I say something, I mean it. I never had to lay hands on her before. She was doing well up until now. Queen wouldn't look at me; she just stared at her plate, pushing her food around. I didn't want tension between us for the remainder of her visit, so I did the only thing I knew would make her forgive me.

Getting up from my seat at the table, I walked over to her. When I placed my hand on her shoulder, her body got tense. *Shit, I really scared her.* I thought to myself. I pulled her chair away from the table and moved to stand in front of her. I lifted her chin up with my finger.

"Baby, look at me please," I said, my voice was soft. I didn't want to give her the impression that I was still mad at her. I needed her to know I was sorry. It took her a minute. I could tell she was thinking it over. Queen always chewed on the inside of her cheek when she was thinking. It was one of the many cute things she did. I remember the first time I noticed it. We were on Oovoo, a video calling app, and she was doing her math homework. I was trying to help her the best I could. Math wasn't one of Queen's strong suits. She struggled with it a lot. But the girl was hella smart. Math just was her kryptonite.

When her eyes finally met mine, I could see the fear in them. I felt bad but not entirely. I was about to be on my Baby Boy type time. Y'all remember the scene where Jody hit Yvette and gave her some head afterwards? Yup, my face was about to be deep in between Queen's thighs.

"Baby, you know me. I would never put my hands on a woman, unless I'm forced." Queen tried to turn her head away from me. I had to keep my composure cause this little attitude of hers was really starting to aggravate me.

"Queen, I'm trying to apologize to you, baby," I said, dropping to my knees. Her shoulders relaxed a little as her eyes were back on me now. I'm telling you a nigga deserved a Grammy for the performance I was about to give.

"I had everything under control and you wouldn't allow me to handle it. I can't have you disrespecting me in my own home. Especially in front of other people." Queen still had nothing but a towel on, which made my job a little easier. I placed both my hands on both her thighs and gently began to rub my thumbs over them.

"I never meant to hurt you, baby. I love you; you know that." Queen rolled her eyes, but she was gonna be feeling the love in a few seconds. Without further hesitation, I pulled her legs apart. I lifted them up to my shoulders and rested them there as I dived face first into her clit. She was already wet with juices. I knew she couldn't resist me. Trying to hold a front like she was mad at a nigga, whole time her pretty little pussy was missing me. I teased her a bit by just blowing on her clit. Queen was starting to squirm, and I put my hands on her hips to keep her in place.

I took her clit into my mouth and sucked on it like it was a jawbreaker. Her breath got caught in her throat, which made me laugh a little. Queen stayed trying to put up a front but deep down, she was just a softie, when it came to me anyway. I continued to suck on her clit, and then I pushed two fingers inside her warm wet tunnel. She was so tight. It was something about knowing I was the only person who has been all up in there. Unlike Brooklyn, who had a few miles.

I continued to finger fuck her and suck on her clit while mumbling, "How sorry" I was. Her moans were like music to my ears. Queen was finally letting her lil attitude go. She was grinding on my fingers and face like she was at a rodeo. I lifted my head from between her thighs and let my fingers do all the work.

"I'm sorry, baby. You forgive me?" I asked her; my voice was gentle as I did.

"Yes...I forgive you," she said in between moans.

"You forgive me?"

"Yes, baby, I forgive you."

"Show me, give me that nut, baby," I coached her as I moved my fingers faster. Queen's moan grew louder as she started to reach her climax. Hell, her cumming wasn't going to be the end of it though. I was rock hard as soon as I tasted her sweet cherry pit.

"Come on, baby. Cum for daddy," I said and started leaving love bites on the insides of her thighs.

"Mmmmhmm." I could feel Queen's wall tightening around my fingers. Within seconds her sweet nectar covered my fingers and dining room chair.

"Good girl," I said as I pulled my fingers out of her and raised them to her lips. Queen opened her mouth and sucked the clean just like I taught her to do. It was something about watching bitches taste themselves that got me off. Hell, I loved that shit. Once she was done sucking the juices off my fingers, I buried my head in her thighs again. I licked all over her pussy, getting every last drop of cum.

Queen always tasted sweet. It took a lot for me to go down on a woman. I didn't have to think twice with Queen though. Like I mentioned before, I was the only nigga hitting this.

After I had my fill of her juices, I kissed her and picked her little ass up. This visit was gonna have more than one happy ending.

Chapter 5

QUEEN

After Ness' apology performance, I tried to forget about what happened. I enjoyed the remainder of the trip. My last night there was when we went to his friend's party. I was in the bathroom getting ready. I was standing in my underwear putting spiral curls in my hair. Ness loved my hair that way. I had it like this the day we met face to face for the first time. So, whenever I knew we were going to be seeing each other, I always had it done to make him happy. I was jamming out to Body Party by Ciara. I was gonna look good. Ness always made sure I was rocking the latest trends. He got me some white distressed jeans from H&M, a Converse sweater with some red low tops Converse sneakers.

The outfit was cute and all, but I didn't deem it party attire. I wanted to show some skin and shake my ass. But Ness said he ain't want no one else to even get a glimpse of what I had to offer. I belonged to him, and no one needed to see what he owned. And although he treated me like I was grown, I was only still sixteen. I didn't have any business showing off my body just yet. I didn't argue with him, so I was gonna wear what he picked out.

When I was done with my hair, I got dressed and did my makeup. I couldn't help but to admire my work in the mirror. I took a few pictures before I exited the bathroom. I was ready for my night out on the town. I was shocked to see that Ness was wearing an outfit similar to mine. But instead of white jeans, he was wearing black, and obviously, his were not distressed.

"There goes my baaaaaby," Ness started to sing when he saw me. He couldn't utter a tune to save his life, but it still made me smile. "Damn, baby, you looking good as fuck right now," he said, walking up to me and giving me a kiss.

"Boy, stop before you mess up my makeup," I said, laughing and pushing him away.

"Makeup? Who you trying to impress?" He asked me. I rolled my eyes.

"I ain't trying to impress anybody. Don't start with that shit. A woman is a reflection of her man. I can go to that party looking busted if you want me to," I teased. He smiled and kissed me again.

"I wonder who taught you that?" He said, tooting his own horn. He didn't respond to the busted thing cause he knew damn well I was not going to be going anywhere looking any ole kind of way.

Once I was ready, we headed out. I was glad the party wasn't at a club or anything cause then I wouldn't be able to drink. But I was finna get fucked up tonight. Ness let me drink with him all the time. I actually had my first drink with him. I can still remember the night it happened. It was a bad night. I had drunk so much I ended up throwing up everywhere. Ness had to take care of me the whole night. He didn't get any sleep.

"Don't think ya lightweight ass getting fucked up tonight. You got a three drink maximum," Ness said as we walked out the door. It was like he was reading my mind. I rolled my eyes.

"Babe, come on, my tolerance has gone up a bit since then," I

26

whined. I wanted to have a good time and be as drunk as everyone else.

"Naw, I'm not falling for that. It's not even about you getting sick. You get too damn violent when you drink." He laughed as we got in the car. I sucked my teeth and didn't respond. I might be a little messy when drinking, but all within good reason. If no one didn't come at me crazy or was trying to be all over my man, everything would be good.

During the drive, Ness let me play DJ. I was pre-gaming in a sense. I wasn't drinking yet, but I was playing my hype playlist. I was all ready for this party. I couldn't sit still in my seat. I was grinding all over it as if it was Ness' face. Hell, if I could stand up in the car, I would have been twerking as well.

"If you don't sit your hype ass the fuck down," Ness yelled over the music. I couldn't help but laugh. He knew I was excited to go out and that I could never hold in my excitement.

"I gotta talk to you on some real shit," Ness said, turning down the music.

"About what, babe?" I asked, finally settling down a bit. He sounded serious, and it had me worried a bit. "You ain't get no bitch pregnant, did you?" My mind immediately went to the worst-case scenario.

"Chill with all that. Ain't no one cheating on your ass," he said with a bit of irritation.

"Mmm... I can't tell," I mumbled under my breath.

"What was that?"

"Nothing. What did you want to talk about?" Ness' side-eyed me because he knew I said something smart. But I guess since he didn't understand what I said, he let it go.

"When we get up in here, don't be acting like a damn fool aight. There's gonna be some females there that might try to throw themselves at me. But at the end of the day, I'm going home with you." I hope he didn't think that was supposed to make me feel better. Like really? Did he not just hear what came out of his mouth? I just nodded. I didn't want to have a repeat of the other day. I just wanted to enjoy the remainder of my stay. If he thought he was gonna be the only one people flocking to, he had another thing coming.

Soon as we got to the party, Ness left me alone. I didn't think it was gonna be like this. I was sure he was gonna want to show me off but apparently not. I sat on the couch by myself sipping on a cranberry and vodka. I hadn't seen Ness yet but fuck it. I didn't care let him stay gone. *Girl, why are you sitting here sulking like it ain't a number of cute brothas in here?* I thought to myself. And I was right. I wasn't gonna let Ness stop me from having a good time. I downed my drink and got up and started to dance. It didn't matter if I was dancing by myself, I was gonna be my own party if anything.

"Yo, look at lil' shawty over there killing it." I heard someone say I just smiled. Knowing damn well they were talking about me. I continued to dance. Just as I was about to stop dancing to make myself another drink, the DJ started playing Bring it Back (Touch yuh toes) by Travis Porter. This was my fucking song! There was no way I was gonna stop dancing now.

Run and hit that pussy like a crash dummy
Bend it over, touch ya toes
Shake that ass for me
Bounce that ass on the flo', bring it back up
Hit a split on the dick, shawty act up

All my practicing was about to pay off. I spent most of my free time in my room watching the Twerk team videos and trying to copy what they did until I had it perfected. I put my hands on my knees, an arch and my back and let my ass shake. Before I knew it, a crowd started to form around me with people cheering me on. Now that I had an audience, I might as well put on a show. I stood up straight before dropping into a full split and humping the floor. I was having a good ass time showing off my twerk skills and no one was about to stop me from having a good time. When the song ended, the crowd was screaming praise at me. Well, mostly the men. The woman just looked on with envy. Not my fault they old asses couldn't move like me. I laughed to myself at the thought as I made my way through the crowd back to the table that had all the alcohol.

"You sure can move that lil' booty of yours." I heard someone say as I was making my drink.

"Ain't nun little about me," I said, turning around to see who had the audacity. To my surprise, it was a tall Rican looking brotha, who had to be at least 6'0. He wore some True Religion jeans with Timbs. A black shirt and a gold Jesus chain. His curly hair was peeking out of the snapback he was sporting. I licked my lips as I let my eyes meet his.

"Lil' booties matter too, ma. I didn't mean any offense," he said, rubbing his hands together.

"Like I said, ain't nun lil about me," I said, mocking him with a smile.

"How old are you? You look a little young to be here."

"I'm old enough. If I wasn't supposed to be here, would you still be here talking to me?" I asked back.

"Aye, don't come at me. I was just asking," he said, with his hands up in the air signaling he ain't want no problems.

"I'm just fucking with you. Chill out, bro," I said, turning my attention back to my drink. We stood at the table talking for a bit when we heard *Work that Monkey* by Kstylis start playing.

"Tryin' to show me what else the lil' booty could do?"

"You asking me to dance?" I asked, looking around to see if I could spot Ness.

"Is that cool wit chu?" I nodded, took his hand, and led him to the middle of the room, It was nice to have some type of attention. I stood in front of him, grinding and shaking my ass on him. I could feel his bulge through his jeans, though he kept trying to adjust so I couldn't feel it.

"Aye Aye Aye!!!! Lil' mama back at it again, folks. And she got a partna this time. I got you, shorty!" The DJ said, which caused all eyes to fall on me and my new friend.

Pop it like a pro started playing, and I was finna go ham. They thought they were amazed by my moves; they didn't see anything yet. Soon as the beat dropped, I was going off. The nigga couldn't even keep up with me. The DJ was hyping me up, so a crowd was starting to form again, and this time I was not getting hate from anyone. I was doing shit you would only see in videos. *MMhmm, that's right, nothing fake over here this is all-natural.* I thought as everyone was watching.

The song had just ended and when I looked out into the crowd, who was standing there staring daggers at me. Fucking Ness. If looks could kill, I'd be dead where I stood. But he wasn't standing alone. That bitch from the other night was there too with her arm laced through his. I rolled my eyes and stormed off, pushing my way through the crowd. I just wanted to get outside to get some air. How that nigga gonna bring me here then leave me for that big bertha looking bitch?

"QUEEN!" Ness was yelling after me, but I just ignored him. I did not want to deal with his ass just yet.

"Bitch! I know you hear me calling your ass!" He screamed as I got out the door. I turned around so fast cause who the fuck did he think he was talking to? I was just about to air his ass out, but as soon as he came outside, He punched me dead in my face. And the light skin bitch was right behind him.

"The fuck you doing dancing on other niggas and shit? Huh?

You fucking disrespectful!" he yelled. The tears were already rolling down my face as I held my cheek.

"Are you serious right now? You left me alone! For what? Her?" I said, pointing to the bitch behind him with my other hand. "I came here to spend time with you, and everywhere I turn, this bitch keeps showing up," I said, my voice was cracking a bit. I knew my face would be swollen later. Hopefully, it would go down some before I made it back home.

"Stay in your lane, little girl. I have no problem dragging your ass up and down the street!" said, stepping closer.

"Brook, shut the fuck up!" Ness yelled.

"Then control your lil baby doll over there. If she wanna be grown, I can beat her ass like she's grown. Shit, someone needs to tear that ass up."

"Bitch, fucking try me! Touch me if you want to. But I guarantee your fat ass is gonna be the one laid out," I snapped back.

"Queen, take ya ass to the car. I'll be there in a minute," Ness said. I no longer had the energy to go back and forth. With tonight being the second time he laid hands on me, I didn't want it to happen a third time. I just couldn't wait for this trip to be over. So, like a little dummy, I took my ass to the car, and waited.

Chapter 6

ANGELICA

It was Sunday and I was sitting downstairs watching Divorce Court waiting for Queen to come home. Clyde was off at the gym, and for that, I was grateful. He did not approve of me watching "Trashy tv" as he calls it. The judge was just about to give her verdict when I heard the front door open.

"I'm home!" Queen yelled as the door shut behind her. I turned the tv off and smoothed out my dress before walking over to the foyer.

"How was your trip?" I asked. I was excited to hear her thoughts on the *Big Apple*. Clyde and I always planned to take her one day but just never got around to it. So, I was happy she was able to go with her school.

"It was cool, mom. As a matter of fact, I'm pretty tired, and I still have to unpack, so I'm going to head up," Queen answered, sounding suspicious and never looking at me head-on. She made her way up the stairs, dragging her suitcase behind her. Something wasn't right, and I couldn't put my finger on it. But my instincts were telling me to follow her, so I did.

"Queen, I wasn't finished talking to you," I said in a stern voice as

I made my way up the stairs hot on her trail. It was obvious something happened while she was away and it was also obvious she was trying to avoid me altogether.

"Mom, I just want to go to sleep, ok? The trip back was super busy and I just want to lay down in my own bed," she protested. I was persistent in finding out what was bothering her, though, so I continued on her trail. Just as I made my way to the landing, Queen shut her bedroom door. This girl must have lost her mind back in NYC, shutting that door while I was talking to her. Yeah, she had to have forgotten who I was. I took a couple deep breaths to calm myself down before this child had me acting out of character. I for damn sure did not knock on her door before entering her room.

"Did you bump your head on the way in here, closing the door in my-" I stopped mid-sentence. Queen was sitting at her vanity and I noticed the right side of her face was swollen. That's what she was hiding when she came in. "...What happened to your face?" I asked her, racing over to her side to expect it myself.

"Mom, it's nothing, ok. I think I might have eaten something with shellfish in it or something I don't know," Queen said, pulling her face away from me.

I gave her that stare that only a mother would know. You know that one that says *I know you're lying.* I did know and I wasn't about to pretend I didn't. If any of those girls from her school were giving her a problem, I didn't have not one problem going in on them and their mamas. They could all see me behind my only child.

"Girl, I know you don't think I believe that. That is not how your body reacts when you eat shellfish. Your throat would have closed, and dad and I would be at your hospital bedside in New York right now. That's why you carry your epi-pen. Try again, little girl. Are any of those hot in the pants girls giving you a problem? You know they are jealous of you cause you are pretty and have all that hair," I went on as I took her chin and turned her face from side to side to examine it more fully.

She tried to snatch away, but I wasn't having it.

"No, mom. It's nothing like that," she protested.

As soon as the words left her mouth, her phone started to ring, and I saw the name "My baby" pop up. I just knew she was lying. She wasn't allowed to have any boyfriends, so seeing that and her face, I hated to, but I put two and two together.

Snatching the phone before she could, I answered with a stern "WHO IS THIS?!"

"I'm sorry, ma'am. I'm looking for Queen," the voice responded. It sounded too damn old to be looking for my baby. I know that for sure.

"The hell you are. Who is this?"

"Mooommm!" Queen protested, reaching for the phone. I gave her the mother of all black mother stares, and she retreated back into herself and looked in the mirror at her own face.

"My name is Ness. I'm just a friend of hers," he told me.

"And how do you know my daughter? How old are you? You damn sure don't sound sixteen." I went in on him.

"I'm sorry if this is a bad time. I'll just try her back later." And he hung up before I could ask anything else.

I dialed the number back and it continued to go to voicemail. This son of a bitch. Turning back to her, I folded my arms and demanded that she start talking.

"Mom, I met him online, okay," she admitted.

"Are you crazy? Meeting people online can get you killed! Did he do that to your face? You better not lie to me either!" I kept going.

"Moom, please, stop...." she begged, tears streaming down her face.

"No, I birthed you and I will be damned if anyone does anything to you that I don't know about. You might not want to talk now, but I ain't stupid. Go downstairs and get an ice pack for your face before your dad gets back and all hell really breaks loose. I'm going to give your ass an hour to pull it together, and when I come back in here, you better be ready to talk about how your face got that bruise and swelling and what really happened this weekend," I warned her as I slid her phone in the pocket of my dress.

She must have forgotten that I was a teenage girl once, and I know what boys want. Hell, her daddy was eight years older than me and I met him when I was thirteen at a carnival. He groomed me for years to be his wife, and I didn't even realize it because of how smooth he was with it. We went from being friends, to him professing his love for me on my eighteenth birthday, to married with her, so I knew the signs. I meant to get to the bottom of this Ness business. I couldn't help but to blame myself for her being attracted to older men. Like mother, like daughter, I guess. I was the reason why Clyde was so adamant about raising Queen so strictly. Because of the age difference between us, he didn't want the same for his lil Queen. Little does he know she was already following in my footsteps.

Chapter 7

QUEEN

I wasn't excited to talk to my mom. How the hell was I supposed to tell her what happened? It would break her heart or worse she would tell my dad. I paced back and forth in my room trying to think. It's not like I can ask Ness what to do since she took my phone with her. Thankfully I knew Ness's phone number by heart, and I had my school laptop. All I had to do was download a texting program, and I could text him. I grabbed my laptop and started to look for a free texting program. Cause I had no idea what to do about the situation at hand.

While waiting for the program to download, I couldn't help but to think about this past weekend. So much has happened I couldn't wrap my head around it. After we got back to his apartment that night at the party, we got into a huge fight about his little whore and me "disrespecting" him. I mean, I never would have ended up dancing with someone else if he didn't leave me alone. In all reality, this entire thing was his fault. But of course, he didn't see it that way. At some point during all that, I ended up apologizing, and we had makeup sex right after. Something in me was telling me to just let him go, but I couldn't bear the thought.

The texting extension finally finished downloading, and I set up my account and texted Ness.

Queen: Hey baby, it's me. Sorry about earlier. My mom was in the room when you called, and I couldn't get to my phone in time.

Ness: I don't have time for the kid shit. Women up and get ya shit together or just don't hmu no more.

What did he mean kid shit? Technically, I was still a kid, and he knew it, so everything that was happening should have been expected.

Queen: Kid shit? Tf is that supposed to mean? You knew what this was from the jump.

Ness: I don't have time for this, Queen. Get ya shit together or don't hit my line like I said.

I didn't text Ness after that. He wasn't going to give me the help I needed to fix the situation. If I couldn't figure out what to tell my mom, I was gonna lose the only person I ever truly loved. I changed into something more comfortable and headed downstairs. I didn't know what I was planning to say to my mom, but if Ness wanted to see how grown I was, I was gonna have to do something.

Once I got downstairs, I looked out the window on the front door to see if my dad's car was in the driveway. Thankfully it wasn't. I walked into the living room, expecting to see my mom sitting on the couch. To my surprise, she wasn't there. It wasn't until I heard her witch cackle that I was able to pinpoint her location. I slowly made my way to the kitchen where she was sitting at the table talking on the phone. I still didn't know what I was gonna tell her. Everyone always said the truth would set you free, right?

It wasn't long before my mom noticed me standing near the refrigerator. She looked me up and down before returning her attention back to whoever was on the phone.

"Girl, let me call you back." My mom hung up the phone and looked at me again.

"So, you ready to tell what really happened over the weekend or we're just gonna keep blaming shellfish?" I took a deep breath and sat down across from her.

It took me about an hour to explain everything to my mom. I started all the way from when my uncle first started touching me till now. Mom was sitting there with a blank expression on her face. Like nothing I said about uncle Deon bothered her.

"Can you at least say something?" I said, looking down at my hands. I was anxious to hear what she had to say. If she had anything to say, that is. The silence was overwhelming. And I was starting to get worried.

"Your father will be home soon. It'll be best for you to avoid him until the swelling goes down." was all she said—not even mentioning the things I said about uncle Deon.

I didn't have the energy to argue, and it seemed like she wasn't going to say anything more on the matter. I got up from the table, grabbed an ice pack from the freezer, and retreated back to my room like I was told. I didn't even ask for my phone back. That was gonna be a whole other argument. Instead, I just unpacked my bags and got ready for the week ahead.

Chapter 8

ANGELICA

Queen had me stuck on what she just told me. There was no way what she said could be true. How could it be? Deon adored her. He would never do anything like that to hurt her. My hands trembled as I tried to process everything. "There's just no way," I said out loud.

"There's no way what?" Clyde's voice broke my thoughts. I was so lost in them I didn't even hear him come into the house.

"What's wrong, dear? Did someone die?" Clyde asked, sitting where Queen once sat. I had to pull myself together. If Clyde found out about this, all hell would break loose in this household. And public enemy number one would be Queen. I put my best smile on and tried to act like everything was alright.

"Everything is fine, dear. There's just no way we ran out of milk. I'm gonna go grab some from the store." I quickly got up from the table and went to the living room to grab my purse and car keys.

"Are you sure everything is alright? I'm having a hard time believing this was over milk." Clyde was hot on my heels. I always had a tough time stopping him from seeing right through me. But I needed answers before I could let him in on this little secret Queen dropped on me. I was able to get Clyde to drop the detective act for now, but I knew I was gonna have to find a better excuse than milk the next time he asked. He was just gonna have to settle for that one for now. I gave him a kiss and went on my way. The drive to Deon's had me on edge. I wasn't even sure what I was gonna say to him; or if he would even confess to the allegations Queen made. Tears filled my eyes as I thought about him violating my baby girl. This just couldn't be true.

I pulled up at Deon's house and sat in the car for about five minutes, trying to get myself together. I pulled out some face tissue from my center console and wiped my face. I didn't need Deon to know I was crying while I was on my over here. I took a deep breath and got out of my car. My nerves were still shaking as I made my way to his front door. I knocked and waited patiently for Deon to answer the door. I knew he was home because his 2014 Cadillac CTS was in the driveway. Just as I was about to knock for the second time, the door swung open.

"What's good, sis? I wasn't expecting to see you today. Is everything good?" Deon asked. I must have woken him up cause he was rubbing his eyes, and his clothes were filled with wrinkles like no one ever taught him how to use an iron. I pushed past him and made my way to the living room without responding. I sat on his sofa and just stared into space, still trying to find the right words to say. How do you bring something like this up? I didn't want to offend him, but who wouldn't get offended being accused of rape?

"Deon...I'm gonna ask you something that might offend you. But I need to know the truth. I have to hear it coming from you," I started. Deon was now standing in front of me. My eyes were focused on the rug. I couldn't dare look at him while asking this question. It hurt me to even have to ask.

"What's going on, Ange? You bugging and it's starting to creep a nigga out." I took another deep breath as I tried to find the courage to say what I had to say.

"Did you touch Queen?" My hands started to shake as the words left my lips. I wanted to puke after speaking them. The thought of him touching my child made me sick to my stomach.

"What the hell do you mean did I touch Queen? What kind of fucking question is that?" The tone of his voice said it all. I knew he would be upset, but I needed to know.

"Earlier today, Queen told me... she told me you have been touching her. For years. Every time you were left alone with her." The tears I thought I dried before exiting my car were back. I could no longer hold back the fear and somewhat anger I was feeling.

"Angelica, don't come up in here with the bullshit. THAT'S MY FUCKING NIECE! THE FUCK I LOOK LIKE TOUCHING HER?" Deon screamed. I didn't know what else to say, or who to believe for that matter. I didn't want to think my own child would lie about something so serious. But then again, she did just try to lie to me about her swollen face. So maybe she would.

"Ange, you know Queen has been a little fresh ass since she turned thirteen. Idk what made her want to tell you some fucked up shit like this. Or what the fuck happened, but she probably been laying down with one of these nappy headed little boys. I didn't touch that girl." I just nodded. Deon adored Queen like she was his own. I couldn't imagine him doing something like that whatsoever. I decided to keep the information I received to myself and not share it with Clyde. I had no way of proving what was told from either side was true or false. For now, it was just better to act as if nothing was ever said to me.

"Why would she even say something like that?" Deon asked, sitting next to me. I finally looked at him. His face was distraught and confused. You can see how much he was hurting from being accused of the accusations. My heart sank more because I did not have an answer for him.

"Does Clyde know about this?" He asked. I shook my head no cause my words would not come to me still. We sat in silence, lost in our own thoughts. After about fifteen minutes, I stood and cleared my throat.

"I should probably get going. I told Clyde I was running to get milk," I said in a low voice. I still had no idea what I was gonna tell him. He wasn't the type of person to just let things go.

"Ok sis, be safe. Also, don't dwell too much on this. You know I love Queen as if she was my own." I nodded and headed out. I stopped at the grocery store, grabbed the milk, and went home. I busied myself with making dinner, and Clyde was in his office, thankfully. I hurried with dinner cause I just wanted to get it done and over with. The only person who would be acting normal would be Clyde. Well, I guess he really wouldn't be acting.

After about an hour, we were all sitting at the table. The tension was so thick you could have cut it with a knife. I guess Clyde noticed the eerie feeling cause he tried to spark up a conversation with Queen about her trip.

"How was the big apple? Did you enjoy yourself?" He asked as he was cutting into his steak.

"It was fine." Queen was giving very vague answers, and Clyde picked up on it. I watched the two go back and forth like a tennis match. You would have thought Queen would be more excited to talk about her trip. But I guess since I kinda intercepted her when she came home, the excitement died down. I wonder how dinner would have gone if I was just the type of parent to not worry about my child. If I hadn't pressured Queen to tell me what happened, what kind of exciting stories would she have told us about her little trip? I guess we may never know.

"Dad, I'm just tired, ok! The play was fine, the trip was fine, everything was fine, damn." The outburst from Queen pulled me away from my thoughts just in time for me to see her storming away from the table and up the stairs. Clyde turned to look at me and I just

44

shrugged. I was not about to clue him in on what was going on. At least for now, I wasn't. I was left alone to clean the mess of dinner by myself, which I didn't mind at all. I was ready for this day to come to an end. Shortly after cleaning the kitchen, I made my way upstairs. I peeked in my bedroom, and Clyde was already asleep. So I went to Queen's room.

"Sweetie, you asleep?" I asked as I peeked into her room.

"No, I'm awake," she said as she sat up in her bed. I walked in and closed the door behind me.

"First off, I don't know what the hell happened at dinner, but you need to apologize to your father in the morning. Your behavior was unacceptable, and I advise you to go to him before he comes to you," I said. Who knew what Clyde would have in mind for punishing this girl? Especially the way she talked to him tonight. He must have thought she lost her damn mind. Queen nodded that she understood and didn't even try to argue her side on why she went off, which was fine with me.

"Secondly, I went to see uncle Deon today. He denied everything. So with that, there's no longer a reason to bring it up anymore. You hear me?" I turned around and was about to take my leave when Queen started going off again.

"This is why I never told you all those years ago! You just can't phantom the thought that your brother touched your little girl! He would never do such a thing! I must be making all this up, right!" Tears were streaming down Queen's face as she yelled. The hurt in her face was evident. The agony in her eyes was so intense it was unbearable for me to see my daughter suffering that way. It was like nothing I've ever seen before.

"What do you want me to do, Queen? How can I believe what you're saying is true? You lied about the trip to New York. Yes, you went, but you lied about the reason. You lied about what happened to your face. Who's to say you're not lying about this? These are serious accusations, Queen. You can ruin a man's life saying things like that. I don't know who to believe. If it really happened, why would you have waited years to finally say something? Now, like I said, we will not speak of this again." I left before she had any time to rebuttal. It hurt my soul to see Queen like that, but she didn't have any evidence proving her statements. There was nothing more I could do about the matter but sweep it under the rug.

Chapter 9

NESS

It's been a couple of days since I heard from Queen. I was a little pressed about it but wasn't going to show it. I didn't have time for the childish games she was trying to play. Hopefully, with this little stunt she was pulling, she was getting her act together. Brooklyn was doing very little to keep my mind from wandering about my baby girl. Usually, Brook was able to ease my mind from any and everything that wasn't her, but today it was not working.

"What's going on with you? You got erectile dysfunction or something? It never takes you this long to get hard when I'm sucking you off," Brook said as she got off her knees and wiped the spit from off the sides of her mouth. She was wearing a teal sheer lace-up bodysuit. Her ass was looking delicious for sure. But my mind was not with it. I had this beautifully built woman standing damn near ass naked in front of me, and I couldn't even stand at attention.

"It ain't nothing you got to worry yourself about. Just keep going; I'm a get there," I said, rubbing my eyes. I had to get Queen off my mind. A nigga was just trying to bust a nut, and I couldn't even do that cause I haven't heard from shorty in a couple days. If I ain't know myself any better, I'd have said I was pussy whipped. But pussy was a dime a dozen, and I didn't have to worry about going on a dry spell.

"I ain't got time for this. You see yourself out," Brooklyn said, walking to her bedroom. Shorty pussy wasn't that good anyway. I got myself together and headed out. I had some errands I needed to run anyhow. Bitches were starting to annoy the fuck out of me today.

I got in my whip and *Loyal* by Chris Brown started blaring through my speakers. I was singing along with it cause that's how I was feeling.

"I wasn't born last night, I know these hoes ain't right. But you was blowin' up her phone last night. But she ain't have her ringer nor her ring on last night, ooh

Nigga, that's that nerve. Why give a bitch your heart when she'd rather have a purse? Why give a bitch an inch when she'd rather have nine?"

I had to admit Queen had me in my feelings for real. Since day one, we talked every single day. This is the first time she just went MIA on a nigga, and I wasn't feeling it all. She had me acting like a bitch nigga, and that wasn't me.

I pulled up to the trap and collected the money that was owed. All I had to do was deliver it to the next lieutenant above me and my job was done. When I got back in the car, I had the idea to pop up on Queen. Well, not really pop up but go down to PA and see why she hasn't been hitting me up lately. I hurried to drop off the money and made my way to Pa. I booked a hotel for the week and everything. I knew Queen's schedule like the back of my hand. I knew what school she went to and what time each class she took started and ended. I even knew the route she took to get home. Now before you start calling me a stalker, let me just explain; Queen willingly gave me this information. She shared everything with me about her life. There were no secrets between us. As far as she knew anyway. But what happened over the weekend when she came to see me might have just tipped her off. Though she didn't say anything about it.

I guess I was pussy whipped. The thought of losing Queen to some little ass boy infuriated me. I have known her since she was eleven. She told me everything. Even though I had my side pieces, none of them could compete with Queen. She was on her own level, and none of the bitches I fucked with could hold a candle to my shawty. My pops always told me if I found a shorty who was down for me, never to let her go. Even if you had to smack the bitch up here and there, they would learn eventually and would always come running back. I couldn't let Queen slip through my fingers. Not after everything we've been through. I taught her everything she knows. Just thinking about her giving my pussy away made me even more upset. I reached for my phone and dialed her number, pressing the speakerphone, so I wouldn't get pulled over for being on the phone.

"Hello...You've reached the voicemail of Queen. I am unavailable to take your call at this time. Please leave your name, phone number, detailed message, and the best time to contact you. I'll be sure to return your call promptly. Thank you!" Mad as hell, I hung up and threw my phone into the passenger seat. She either blocked my number or was forwarding me to voicemail. I was not a leave a voicemail type of nigga. Queen for damn sure knew to answer the phone when I called. And If she couldn't talk, her ass knew to text me about the reason way beforehand. It was still early in the day, so I should make it to PA around the time she got out of school. Which was perfect. I could park outside her school to see what she was up to and follow her from there.

Just as expected, I was able to park a good distance away from her school just before she got out. When I touched down in PA, I rented a different car so she wouldn't get suspicious. I was mad as hell sitting in this 2014 Toyota Corolla. But I had to do what I had to do. I looked at my phone, and it was three on the dot. Kids would be rushing out the doors any minute now. I never thought I would be this type of person but she had me all types of fucked up. I was so lost in my thoughts I didn't even notice that the parking lot was starting to fill with kids. I leaned forward so I could see better and I noticed her right away.

Queen had her hair in pin curls with the hairpins still in. Wearing a pair of black distressed jeans with a skin tight white t- shirt and the black and white Jordans I got for her. She was walking with two other girls. I wasn't really paying them any mind.

"Who the fuck is this nigga?" I asked myself as I watched some young nigga came running up behind Queen and hug her from behind. I was bout ready to hop out this fucking car, until I seen Queen squirm out they grasp.

"Yeah, that's my baby. Let them know who daddy is," I said to myself as I continued to watch the interaction. Queen smacked the young nigga in the back of the head before throwing her arms around his neck. This bitch thought I was playing with her. She out here hugging niggas now, that's what we doing? I took my phone out and took a picture of the little whore betraying me. After everything I ever did for her, she wanted to leave me for some lil ass boy. We'll see about that.

I followed Queen home. She walked with the girl and the little nigga for a bit before they all went their separate ways. Not once did Queen pull out her phone. Which was odd. Because she was always on it. Any time she wasn't around her folks, she was texting or calling me. So the sudden change was not like her at all. Queen ended up going straight home. I parked three houses down and sat that way for almost four hours before driving back to the hotel. I had to figure out who the hell this little nigga was.

When I got back to my room, I tried calling Queen again, and just like before, I got her voicemail. Only this time, I left her a message.

"Listen here, lil' girl. I don't know what type of games you are playing, but you gonna get ya self hurt. You better fucking call me for real." And with that, I hung up the phone.

. . .

It was Friday. I followed this girl all week, and it was always the same damn thing. After school Queen would be walking with one of her female friends, and then the young boul would pop up, covering her eyes from behind, and she would laugh. After that, she would just go home. I still haven't heard from her either. Today that was all gonna change. After she was three blocks away from the school, I pulled right up on that ass.

"Queen, get your ass in this car now!" I yelled from the window. She jumped before looking over at me. A big ass smile on her face, like she didn't do anything wrong. She had no idea what trouble she was in. Queen walked around to the passenger side and got in. I didn't look at her once. She put her book bag in the passenger seat and closed the door.

"What are you doing here? And where's your truck?" She asked as I pulled off. I simply turn the stereo up and let the sounds of Dej Loaf's *Try Me* drown her out. My first reaction was to fuck her up right there in the car, but I held back and decided to wait 'til we got back to my room. Queen must have picked up on the vibe cause she kept her mouth shut the entire ride and just stared out the window. That was in her best interest. Anything she could have said could have made this situation a whole lot worse for her ass. I pulled up to the telly and jumped out of the car with quickness. Speed walking to the passenger side, I opened her door and snatched her out.

"What the fuck, Ness!?" She exclaimed as she tried to pull away from me.

"Now's not the time for your fast ass to be getting tough. Get your damn bag," I said through gritted teeth. I didn't loosen my grip on her at all. She just looked at me with confusion before shutting the door and opening the backseat door to get her book bag. I dragged her ass all the way back to my room. She tripped a few times from trying to match my pace. I didn't give a damn. Hell, if she would have fallen, I would have let her stupid ass.

After we got to the room, I let her go. Queen made her way to the bed and I just paced back and forth. I was fuming.

"You going to tell me what this is all about? Like you gripping me up and shit showing up unannounced?" This bitch must have been out of her damn mind. That whole sentence made me snap. When I tell you I crossed the room so fast, niggas would have thought I was the flash himself. I backed handed her so hard she fell off the bed.

"Bitch! Unannounced? Maybe I could have let your stupid ass know if you would have returned a nigga phone calls. But no, your fast ass out here fucking with that little nigga at your school!" I was standing over her at this point. She looked up at me and her lip was busted.

"What are you even talking about?" She asked as she dabbed at her lip with her finger.

"Don't play with me. bitch!" I screamed. I grabbed a fist full of her hair and delivered blow after blow to her face. "You thought you could play me? Huh? You thought I wouldn't find out. I followed your ass all week I seen you with the nigga. Then you have the nerve to not call or text me? Bitch, are you out of your mind!" I finally stopped hitting her after I tired myself out. She laid on the floor in a fetal position crying.

I walked over to my duffle bag and got my weed and a wrap, and started to roll up. I needed to calm my nerves before I killed this bitch. She had me all types of fucked up.

"Get the fuck up off the floor and go clean yourself up," I said as I took a hit of the blunt. Seems like I wasn't training this hoe good enough if she thought she could play a nigga like me.

"You're so damn ungrateful. After everything I did for you and this how you repay me? It's a damn shame. You don't realize how good you have it. What can that other nigga do for you, huh? Not a damn thing." I took another hit and let the weed do its thing.

"Queen, don't make me repeat myself. You look pathetic," I said, looking down at her. Queen lifted herself slowly off the floor. She was still sniffling. I bet she learned her lesson now.

"You can't just throw me to the side, Queen. I don't know what that lil' nigga been telling you. But the only way you can get rid of me is if I'm dead." Queen grabbed her book bag and made a beeline towards the bathroom. She didn't even bother to look at me, which didn't bother me. She can have her little ass attitude all she wants. She had no one to blame but herself.

After about fifteen minutes, she walked out of the bathroom. She did a good ass job cleaning herself up. Didn't even look like she got her ass beat.

"Come here, baby girl," I said with my arm outstretched. Queen was hesitant at first, but she came like she was told. I grabbed her by the waist gently and sat her on my lap, "You know I don't like hurting you, baby. But you need to realize how good you have it with me. I love you, baby girl. I really do. And I need you to know that. And I hit you to teach you. There's just things you should and shouldn't do." I kissed her on the cheek and patted her thigh. "Now get your things. I'm gonna take you home. And when we get there, let me do the talking. Understand?" Queen nodded, all the while staring straight ahead. "That's my girl."

Chapter 10

CLYDE

I was sitting in my study with a man who claimed to be dating my sixteen year old daughter. It was obvious he was not a high school student, so how he became acquainted with my little girl was beyond me. I didn't know what to think of this. I was shocked to see him standing in my foyer holding hands with Queen. To my surprise, Queen didn't do the introductions. She stood next to him as quiet as a field mouse and allowed him to do the talking. Although I have instilled in Queen that women should be seen and not heard, I knew my child, and Queen wasn't the type to stand idle in the shadows and let a man take the lead. She was a very opinionated individual. She always made sure she was heard, no matter the circumstances. To see her finally practicing the lessons I've been giving her since she could comprehend, should have made me happy. Although, for some reason, it was actually unsettling.

"I know this may come to you as a shock, Mr. Davis, but I can assure you that my love for your daughter is real." I wasn't sure what to say to this man. or what he wanted me to say. Angelica pulled me to the side shortly after they arrived and explained to me what happened in New York. So not only did I have a grown ass man in my house, who said he loves my teenage daughter. I also had a man who apparently laid hands on my daughter sitting across from me as if he had her best interest at heart.

"Ness, is it? Can you explain to me what happened in New York between you and my daughter?" As angry as I was, I believed myself to be a reasonable man. There were two sides to every story. I had to at least give him the chance to tell his side.

"Oh, about that," The young man started off. I had to cut him off before he started trying to feed me some bullshit ass story.

"Listen here, Ness. I'm not a fool. I highly encourage you to think about what story is about to leave your mouth. I can assure you that I don't have stupid written across my forehead." He nodded in understanding.

"Well, sir, to tell you the truth, Queen came to see me in New York. While she was in the bathroom, I had an unexpected visitor from my past. I tried to handle the situation when Queen came out running that mouth of hers. And with her being your daughter, I'm sure you can understand how that went." I sat listening to what he had to say. Making sure to hear every last detail to be sure not to miss anything before casting judgment.

"I told Queen to go back to the room and let me handle it; she did not. So yes, I did strike her across the face for being disobedient. Now before you say anything, Mr. Davis. Please allow me to say this. I love your daughter more than anything. I'm not the type of man who just goes around hitting women. But a slap here and there to get them in line won't hurt them, am I right?"

Surprisingly, I agreed with Ness one hundred percent. Seems to me he was just teaching Queen how to be an exceptional woman. Queen was a hard one to tame, even as her father. I had a hard time keeping her in line, so I understood where Ness was coming from. Queen's mouth always got her in trouble one way or another, so a slap to the face was hardly anything. There were times I even had to strike Queen because of that mouth of hers. So I understood where this young man was coming from completely.

"Well, Ness, technically, Queen is not supposed to be dating right now. And from the information you gave me about how you've been seeing my daughter for a year now, I'd hate to break up a happy couple. It doesn't seem like you been a distraction to her studies. Although I'm not a fan of the age difference. I have a feeling you might be good for Queen." I was gonna keep a close eye on this Ness character. I wholeheartedly meant everything I said to him.

"I already know trying to keep you apart will only push her more in your direction." With that being said, I shook his hands. Yes, I shook hands with a man who laid hands on my child. But I had a feeling he was just what Queen needed.

Chapter 11

ANGELICA

Queen and I were in her room as the men were talking. Soon as I closed the door behind me, she burst into tears. I figured it had something to do with the man downstairs talking with her father. I had no idea what was going on. I was shocked to see her walking in the house with this grown ass man. But if my intuition serves me correctly, this was the man who had my baby's face all swollen.

"Baby, what's wrong?" I asked her, sitting on her bed next to her. I pulled her into me and tried to comfort her as best as I could.

"He did it again, mom. This time worse than before," Queen started. She pulled away from me as she continued her story. "It's your fault!" She screamed as she got up to get away from me. Now I was puzzled on how her getting hit was my fault.

"What do you mean? How is any of this my fault? And watch your tone speaking to me, young lady." Queen's face was twisted up and her eyes, although full of tears, showed a burning hatred for me.

"If you didn't take away my phone, he wouldn't have shown up here. Ness thinks I was ghosting him because I haven't contacted him all week, and I couldn't do that because YOU had my phone. So yea, this ass whoopin' I had to endure before coming here was all on you." I was taken aback. Like did this child not hear me when I told her to watch her tone? If she thought the beating she took was bad, she was gonna be in a world of hurt talking to me like I was one of her little friends.

"Queen Davis, I'm not gonna say it again. Watch your damn tone. I'm not one of your friends, you hear? As far as trying to place the blame on me, you have been mistaken. Your phone got taken away because you lied. Not me. Having a phone is a privilege, not a right. Last time I checked, your father and I paid the bill for this, not you. So I'll take it whenever I please." This girl must have lost her damn mind talking to me like that. Hell, I was trying to be on her side, but if you asked me, Ness didn't beat her good enough. I was subjected to the same thing Queen was going through.

When I first met her father, I had to endure multiple beatings. Each one turned me into the woman I was today. The perfect trophy wife. Obedient, caring, and doting. That was the formula for the perfect wife, was it not? I never wanted Queen to suffer the same fate as I, but since she wanted to be grown, she was going to have to learn on her own.

"Listen up, Queen. You wanted to be grown and be with a grown ass man, so this is what comes with it. Sometimes you get smacked up. You either learn from it or it continues to happen." I got up off her bed and left the room. There was no more I could say to her.

Chapter 12

QUEEN

It was my eighteenth birthday, and I was planning to turn the fuck up with my girl Brielle I had met at work. Brielle was twenty years old, but she was cool. Even invited me to have my party at her house and she would pay for all the liquor. Even though we haven't known each other for long, she has become my best friend. She knew more about me than my parents did. Brielle was a party girl. If there was any party to go to, Brielle was the first to know about it. Which is why I was so grateful she offered to host my party. If it wasn't for her, I would have been stuck in the house with my parents and uncle Deon and we all know how that could have gone.

I was sitting in Brielle's room. Meek Mill's *House Party* could be heard blaring from the downstairs. I definitely needed this party. I just broke up with Ness about two weeks ago and got my number changed. I haven't been with anyone but him. He was my first and only for everything. But that wasn't the case with him. Brielle drove me up to his place one of the weekends we were off. and this nigga had the nerve to be laid up in the house with the same bitch from the first time I ever went to his house. Like how the fuck you want me to be one hundred percent loyal to your ass, but you fucking every hoe that cross ya path.

Ness had me fucked up. So I was gonna get fucked up and fucked tonight. Why shouldn't I celebrate my newfound freedom? My hair was curled and I was rocking the dress that broke the internet a few weeks before. I didn't see what the fuss was about. The dress was clearly white and gold. I texted Brielle to let her know I was ready to make my entrance. I was hype to be sporting the new Iphone 6+ courtesy of my parents. Soon as it came in my possession, I had my number changed so Ness couldn't reach me. The only thing I didn't block him on was Snapchat so that way I could be sure he knew I was living my life and not thinking about him. I wanted him to see my stories tonight, so I was damn sure gonna act up.

Once I heard Tyga's *Happy Birthday* playing, I got my ass up, did a quick look over in the mirror, and made my way to where the party was.

"HAPPY BIRTHDAY, BITCH!" Brielle screamed as I was walking down the steps. Those who were near stopped to tell me happy birthday as well. Brielle walked up to me carrying two shots; tonight was finna be popping.

After a couple drinks, I was wildin' out. I was dancing with some cutie. He was light skin with green eyes, and his lay was on point. I could feel his bulge on my ass as I was grinding on him. Brielle had my phone taking videos for my Snapchat. I knew Ness' ass would be pissed, but that was the point. I didn't have my eye on anyone else but the nigga I was dancing with. Yeah, this the nigga I was gonna be throwing my panties at later tonight. The song ended and I was out of breath. I was throwing my best moves at him and he was able to keep up.

"That ass had me mesmerized, shawty. Like damn," he said as he smacked me on my butt. I giggled.

"You have to be extra nice to me tonight. I am the birthday girl," I said, moving closer to him. A smile appeared on his lips and I couldn't help but think how good he was at going downtown.

"Oh, so you're the birthday queen everyone is talking about?"

"Birthday queen, you better put some respect on my name. It's Queen; nice to meet you." He busted out laughing.

"Oh shit, your *name* is Queen? That's tight." I smiled and nodded as the realization hit him. "Well, Queen, how about we get another drink in you?" I agreed; I watched the sexy stranger walk off into the crowd. I was biting my lower lip as I was thinking about the possibilities of the end of the night.

"BITCH!" Brielle screamed, pulling me out of my fantasy. I turned my attention to her drunk ass. "Ness is pissed off. He's been sending you snaps all night. Especially after he watched the story with light skin." I couldn't help but laugh. That nigga was all up in his feelings. Niggas can never handle when we do the shit they do to us to them. I had Ness right where I wanted him.

"Girl, I knew he was gonna do that. With his bitch ass. Want to be out fucking and licking every got damn thing. But let me dance on a nigga and it's a problem. Bitch, I'm single and I need to experience more than just Ness dirty dick ass." Just as me and Brielle was giving each other a high five, my sexy stranger returned with our drinks and shots,

"Devon, let me find out you're trying to get my girl fucked up," Brielle said jokingly.

"It's not even like that, Bri. I'm just trying to make sure the birthday girl is having a good time." I happily accepted the shot and the drink.

"Bottoms up!" I yelled before downing both. The DJ started playing *She Gotta Donk* by Soulja Boy, and the crowd started going wild. Even though the song was a few years old, we were all turnt up. I turned my ass around and started twerking on Devon. This was by far my favorite birthday and it was all thanks to Brielle.

. . .

By three o clock, the party came to an end, and people started to bounce. Devon and I were sitting on the couch while Brielle was kicking people out.

"Y'all don't gotta go home, but y'all gotta get the fuck up outta here. I know that for damn sure," Brielle said. As she was going through the house finding those who thought this was about to turn into a massive sleepover. Devon and I were just laughing. We were drunk and high off our ass.

"A ke ke ke! I'm glad y'all two think it's the fuck funny. Get y'all asses up and help, the fuck. Y'all bout to be next." Devon and I just laughed harder at Bri's frustration. We got up and helped her get the remainder of the stragglers out. Once we were sure we had everyone out, we cleaned up a bit and retired upstairs. Brielle had a guest bedroom which me *and* Devon were going to be occupying.

"Don't do anything I wouldn't do," Brielle said before closing her door.

"Bitch, that ain't much,," I yelled back, laughing. I closed the door to the guest bedroom and Devon was already sitting on the bed rolling up.

"How high do you think you can get?" I asked, teasing him. "Hell, we just smoked not that long ago. At this point you just wasting weed, my nigga," I said, sitting next to him.

"You're doing all that talking like you ain't planning to hit this," Devon said as he lit the blunt.

"That's not the point," I said, laughing. I was checking my Snapchat and saw that Ness watched every last story from the party. I smirked. I opened the snaps he sent, which were just threats and I laughed.

"What got you over there geeking?" Devon asked as he passed me the blunt. I shook my head.

"Nothing important, just my ex mad as hell." Devon passed me the blunt and I took a hit. He took my phone out my hand and sat it on the nightstand.

"Enough about your ex; tonight's supposed to be about you. So why don't you lay back and let me make you feel good." Devon gently pushed me back on the bed. I was still pulling on the blunt but I was gonna let him rock out. He spread my legs apart and pulled my panties down. I had to help him out by lifting my ass. He placed soft kisses up my thighs before devouring my pearl. In comparison to Ness, Devon's techniques had a bitch's leg quivering. I was in heaven. The mixture of the weed and the feeling of getting my pearl licked was enough to put me in a dopamine coma. Tonight was gonna end happily. Well, that is if his dick game was on par with his head game.

Chapter 13

NESS

I swear Queen has been testing me lately. Just because she caught me with a shawty. It was her fault for popping up unannounced. Like I told her about that shit on several occasions. Her ass wouldn't have her panties in a twist if she would have let a nigga know she was finna slide through. Bitch broke her own heart, on God. Now she out here thinking she *single,* posting snaps with this Chris Brown wannabe. I swear on everything, let that bitch give my pussy away, and we're gonna have some serious problems. Only nigga that should be sliding up in that is me and me only. I didn't give a fuck if I ended up dropping her; I should be the only one hitting that. Hell, if she really wanted me out of her life she would have tried blocking me on snap too. This wasn't her first time doing some shit like this either. She even changed her number on me a few times. Thankfully Clyde always had my back.

Queen obviously wanted me to see her show her ass. Well two can play that game. I was gonna give her a pass since it was her birthday, but she had me fucked up grinding on this nigga. This is the game she wanted to play, say less then.

I texted her dad. Yup, I sure did. Call me what you want. I'm just trying to protect what's rightfully mine. I already knew her dad ain't play that shit. After our first encounter, I actually grew close to her fam. We had an understanding. So yup, I let her pops know what was up. He assured me he was gonna handle it when she got home. I had to press the issue. I couldn't screenshot her snaps cause the app would let her know I did. So I couldn't really send proof . But I insisted that he pull up to wherever she was at and drag her ass home. Knowing Queen, she would want to get back at a nigga. And I had to kill that shit before the pretty boy got a taste. Clyde gave in and told me he was gonna get her home. Queen had obviously forgotten who she belonged to.

"Baby, get off your phone. What got you so tense anyway? Please don't tell me you still after that little ass girl," Brook said, wrapping her arms around my neck.

"I told you about speaking on shit you don't know about, shawty." I had to remind her what her place was. It was hard keeping all these bitches in line. I didn't see how pimps did it. I had to salute them for putting up with such bullshit. I was doing the damn thing, though. I put my phone down and gave Brooklyn the attention she wanted. That was the only reason Brooklyn ever stepped out of line. She was an attention whore. Let her be in my presence, and my attention was elsewhere, she knew how to reverse that. She came close to crossing the line a few times, but she knew better. Hell, maybe I need her to teach Queen. Queen was proving hard to break as she got older. Developing opinions and shit. Sometimes a headstrong woman is attractive when they know their place. Queen was headstrong and stubborn, and the older she got, the more stubborn she became. She was gonna learn eventually. I been telling her for years now the only way she would get rid of me is if one of us died. And I'm telling y'all now it was not gonna be me.

Seeing as though I couldn't get Queen out of my head, I had to cut things short. It was a good thing I was only in Maryland. I was an hour away from Queen. I brought Brook with me just so I wouldn't have to go looking for entertainment. Getting pussy was not an issue. Finding good pussy was.

"Listen, Brook. I'm gonna head out. I have something I need to handle," I said as I stood up. I grabbed my pants from off the floor and pulled them on.

"Where are you going?" Brook asked, starting to get out of the bed.

"Don't worry about it. Stay your ass in this room." I grabbed my car keys and headed out. I don't know what was coming over Brook lately. She was my business bitch. The bitch I took with me to go handle things. I wasn't big in the drug game, but I was in it. And if I crossed anyone, they would go to the person closest to me. If they always see Brook, they would think she was my shorty. I guess, in a sense, she was. But she wasn't my main. It's fucked up for sure. But I be damned if something happens to my Queen. I treated her like shit and wasn't always faithful, but I took care of her. I loved her for sure. It might not look like I did cause I had my own special way of showing it. Even if Queen herself failed to realize that.

Chapter 14

QUEEN

I was fuming. You know how embarrassing it is to have your dad drag you out of someone's house in nothing but a towel? All my shit was still at Brielle's crib. Including my phone and car keys. I sat in the passenger seat, arms crossed, looking out the window. My dad was going off about how I was raised better than this, and everything him and mom sacrificed for me. You know the usual bullshit parents say when you get in trouble. I wasn't listening to a damn thing he was saying. Ever since he found out about Ness, me and my dad were always butting heads. We couldn't go more than three days without arguing. And every week, I was put out the house. Or as he likes to say, I "ran away."

I fell back from my parents, if I'm being honest. It all started after they finally met Ness. I'm lying, sorta, I fell back from my mom after I told her about Deon ass, and she didn't believe me. And even after I told her, Deon still touched me every now and again. I can admit my mother has been limiting the time he is at the house without her or my dad, or both being present. But limiting the time he's around me didn't stop him from touching me whenever the opportunity arises. I fell back from my dad after they met Ness. It was like ever since that day, we were constantly fighting. Like all the time. And whenever something happened between Ness and me, my dad would believe his ass over his own daughter. So in my mind, I didn't even have parents. Only person I had in my corner was Brielle. And that's probably why we were as tight as we were.

Brielle didn't have the type of childhood I did. She had it worse. She was in and out of foster homes since she could remember. At every foster home she was at, she was abused one way or another. I was all she had as well. She didn't even know who her parents were. Apparently, her mother left her at the hospital a month after she was born. It's fucked up cause maybe Brielle didn't have to go through all this shit if her mom would have kept her. She didn't know why her mother gave her up. So, on the other hand, maybe things could have been a lot worse. Brielle tries to think of it as her mother saving her from an even worse hell. She always said, "Maybe the life she was living wasn't suitable for me to be around. And even though I've been through some shit, it might have been better than the shit I would have gone through if she would have kept me."

I always felt bad after I complained about the little shit I went through with my parents to Brielle. At times I forget she doesn't even know her parents. At least mines are still here, right? I mean, yea they be on some other shit, but they here.

I still couldn't believe my dad really dragged me out in nothing but a damn towel. Like, did he really think this was gonna make it any better? Well, he didn't really spoil my fun. Cause I still got what I wanted at the end of the night. I smirked, thinking about my light skin stranger. Man, when I tell you that nigga was hung! Chile, up until this point I only had sex (Consensual sex, might I add) with Ness. I didn't realize what I was missing. Ness got the job done. But after experiencing someone new, I finally had something to compare it to. Ness couldn't hold a candle to Devon. He was hitting spots I didn't even know existed. I wasn't a runner by any means, but boy, did that nigga have a lot of dick, and he filled me up with every inch of it. I wasn't able to handle it.

"Queen! You are not even listening to me. Are you?" The sound of my name pulled me out of my wonderful thoughts. I rolled my eyes before responding.

"No, I'm not. I'm officially eighteen now, a legal adult. I don't have to listen to anything you say, honestly." I shifted my position in the seat, not giving a flying rat's ass about what my father thought of me.

"See, that's your damn problem. You think just because you're considered an adult that makes you grown. Well, sorry to burst your bubble, sweetheart; it doesn't. Until you're living on your own and paying your own bills, you're not grown. As long as you're living under my roof, you are a child and will be treated as such." Here he goes with the living under his roof bullshit again. One day I'm just gonna pack my shit and be out. I'm not gonna leave a note or anything. Just leave.

We pulled up to the house, and to my surprise, Ness was standing in the driveway.

"What the hell is he doing here?" I threw out loudly.

"Queen, language. You have a better vocabulary than that," my father said as he turned off the car. Ignoring him, I climbed out the car, still holding my towel up and walked right over to Ness.

"What the fuck are you doing here? It's over or can you not understand that?" I didn't care that my dad was still standing outside with us. I wanted to know why this nigga was standing in my driveway.

"Queen, I'm not gonna tell you again-"

"Tell me what, dad? Watch my mouth? Don't talk to my boyfriend like that? Well, guess what, dad. If you didn't have your head so far up Ness' ass, you would have known that I broke up with him. He cheated on me. But you don't care about that. You believe everything he tells you and then some." By this time my mother was walking out of the house. I was screaming, and I didn't give a damn about the neighbors. My parents always wanted to put up the front of how we were the perfect family. Which was far from true. The family secrets, the verbal abuse, we had it all. So, I wanted everyone to see the Davis's as we truly are.

"Queen, honey, why don't we take this inside? We have neighbors, for crying out loud." My mom walked over to me and placed her hand on my lower back and tried to guide me to the front door. "Why are you only in a towel, sweetie?"

I snatched away from my mother, and just as I was about to open my mouth, my father spoke.

"She's in a towel because for some reason in her head, we raised a whore." Tears started to fill my eyes. It was nice to finally know what my father thought of me.

"I'm a whore now?! How am I a whore, daddy? Because I decided to sleep with another man? I am single. What part of that don't you get?" At this point, I was ready to lay everything out on the table. "Oh! I think I know how I became a whore, daddy. Why don't you ask mom? Hmm. Ask mom how I came to her after I went to New York and told her uncle Deon has been touching me for years! Oh, but we don't want to talk about that, right? There's just no way he could do such a thing to the niece he loves like his own child." My vision was blinded by the tears in my eyes. I had dished out all our dirty laundry in the driveway where all our neighbors could hear. Now there was nothing left to do but actually talk about this. There was no way they would just sweep it under the rug this time.

"What do you mean Deon touched you? Angelica, is this true? You knew about this?" My dad was now focused on my mother.

"Clyde I-"

"Save it! I think enough has happened here tonight. I think it's best for us to all go to bed and talk about everything in the morning." He stopped her with his decree.

THE MAKINGS OF QUEEN

I didn't have an issue with that at all. I sashayed my ass to the door. Just as I was about to walk in the house, I felt someone grab my hand.

"Can I talk to you?" Ness said before I even turned around. I thought about it for a minute. Everything in me was telling me to say no, but I gave in.

"If you must, but I've been standing outside in a towel long enough. We can take this inside," I answered curtly, snatching my arm away from him. I was still pissed at him, but I was gonna at least hear what sorry excuse he came up with this time.

This wasn't the first time I caught Ness cheating. Nor was it the first time we broke up either. It's been happening more and more often. It was like he thought I was stupid. Like I wouldn't find out about his little flings just because he lived in another state. Funny thing is he did most of the shit while I was with him. Like how stupid can you be? Flirting with other girls while you're with your girlfriend. Just pathetic.

I was headed up the stairs and I heard footsteps behind me. It couldn't have been my parents because I could still hear them talking outside.

"Where do you think you're going?" I asked Ness as I turned around.

"You said we could talk; I was just following you," Ness answered me with a smirk. I rolled my eyes.

"Talking is the only thing that will be happening," I said, as I turned to go back up the stairs. Little did I know, I was dead wrong.

Chapter 15

NESS

I never hit Queen while we were at her house. Out of respect for Clyde, of course. But seeing her get out of the car in nothing but a towel set me off. I knew what to expect from Clyde telling me. But I didn't think it was actually true. I closed and locked the door behind us once we entered her bedroom. I didn't even know where to begin. I was conflicted. I was mad as hell at her, but looking at her in that towel had my soldier standing at attention.

"What you want to talk about? Cause I have nothing left to say to you," Queen informed me as she walked over to her dresser.

Pulling open the third drawer to grab an oversized t-shirt. I licked my lips as I watched her drop her towel and pull the shirt over her frame. I swear this girl was blessed with the perfect body proportions. Her ass didn't take away from her tits, and vice versa. She was already a double D and had an ass most women had to go get a Brazilian butt lift to have. Her body would make any man go crazy.

I pulled my phone out. I had 20 texts from Brook. I ignored them and texted Brielle. I got her number from Queen's phone a while ago thinking it would come in handy, and sure enough, it did. Seeing as though Clyde picked Queen up, I was sure she had left all her shit there. I sent Brielle a quick text telling her to drive Queen's car to the house in the morning and bring anything else she may have left there. Like I don't know, her damn clothes.

"HELLO?! You said you wanted to talk and I don't hear any talking." Queen's voice came crashing through my thoughts as I looked up and saw her standing in front of me. "Let me guess; you're texting that bitch." I couldn't help but smile. Seeing her get so worked up was cute. For someone who claimed they were single, she sure did care about what a nigga was doing.

"Listen, I'm gonna give you a one-time pass because it's your birthday. You wanted to show your ass, cool. I'm not even gonna comment on why ya pops had to bring you home in a towel." Queen crossed her arms over her chest and rolled her eyes. "But seeing how you all mad cause you *think* I'm texting a bitch, tells me you're not really over me. Are you?" I placed my hands on her thighs and slowly started inching my way up under the shirt she was wearing.

"You're giving me a pass? Ha, I don't need a pass from you. You cheated on me time and time again. I'm done with yo-" Queen stopped mid-sentence. I smiled.

She lost her train of thought soon as I reached her pearl. I was using my index finger to draw small circles on it. Worked every time. While my one hand was busy playing with her pearl, my other hand made its way to her ass. I had big hands, and yet they were not big enough to cup one of her cheeks. Her ass was just that big. I smacked her ass and started squeezing it. Queen was starting to hunch over like her legs were ready to give out any minute.

"Now like I was saying, I'm giving you a pass because it's your birthday. Do some dumb shit like this again, and I promise you'll regret it. You understand?" I smacked her ass harder than I did before to get my point across.

"Yes... I understand."

"Yes, who?" I slapped her ass again.

"Yes, daddy." I took my finger off her clit and inserted two fingers inside of her pussy. I couldn't help but think she didn't put panties on for this exact reason. Queen sometimes forgets I know her more than she knows herself. It was easy to get her to change her mind if you knew how. I continued to finger her until she burst all over my hand.

"Now show me how sorry you are," I said as I pulled my fingers out and brought them to my lips. Without hesitation, Queen kneeled in front of me and started to unfasten my jeans. Once my dick was released from its confines, Queen went to town. I'm not talking just sucking on it. She was slobbering on it like she was dying of thirst, and my dick contained the only water for miles around. She used her tongue, deepthroated right off the bat, and everything was very wet and slippery.

"Yea, show daddy how sorry you are," I said as I placed my hand on the back of her head. I had to give it to Queen, when we first met she didn't know how to do anything. Even with her bitch ass uncle touching her at a young age, you would have thought he would have taught her some shit. I was happy to take the role as teacher for her. I taught her everything she knew. I taught her how to please me. Which is why I always get so upset when she tries to pull shit like this. I wasn't gonna have her out here doing what she do for me for some other nigga. That shit was dead, on God. With the way she was sucking my shit, I knew I had my baby back, no doubt about it.

Chapter 16

BRIELLE

When I woke up the next morning, I was shocked to find Devon alone in my guest bedroom. That was odd. *I knew I left them both here last night.* I thought to myself. Last night's events were hazy. I couldn't remember much. And when I tried to, my head would start pounding.

"Fuck it! I don't have time for this." Just as I was about to leave the room, I noticed Queen's phone and car keys on the bedside table. I grabbed them and left. She had to be in the house somewhere if she left her phone and didn't have her keys. I searched the entire house and couldn't find her anywhere. I walked back to my room and grabbed my phone. Someone must have known where she went. When I unlocked my phone, I had a text from an unknown number,

Unknown sender: Drive Queen's car back to the house. I'll make sure you can get back home. Also, bring anything else she may have left with you.

What type of sick shit is this? I didn't know what was going on, but I wasn't gonna head over there by my damn self. Oh, I was definitely going. I had to figure out what happened to my girl. I hurried to get dressed and went back to my guest room to wake Devon up. I was so focused on trying to figure out where Queen was it didn't even cross my mind to ask him if he knew.

"Devon! Devon, wake your ass up!" I yelled, throwing a pillow at him.

"Ughh, what and why?" Devon mumbled, pulling the covers over his face.

"Nigga, if you don't get your ass up!" I pulled the covers off him, which I immediately regretted. I had forgotten Queen and him was doing they thing last night.

"Where is Queen!" I yelled as he grabbed a pillow to cover himself.

"I don't know. Someone knocked on the door last night after we got out the shower. When we answered it, there was some old head standing there. He ended up dragging her out the house, and they got into a white Mercedes Benz and left." I couldn't believe what I was hearing. Did this nigga just tell me my friend was kidnapped?

"Did you try to stop them?" I asked.

"No, the fuck I look like Captain save a hoe?" Devon said, getting out the bed and gathering his clothes.

"Boy, you [bout to get ya self fucked up, keep testing me. Hurry up and get dressed. I need you to ride with me somewhere." I picked Queen's clothes up off the floor as Devon was getting himself together.

"Note to self; disinfect the guest room after I find Queen," I said to myself.

Thirty minutes later, we were at Queen's front door. I was banging on the door like I was the damn police. I wasn't playing any games. And I was gonna continue banging on the door until someone got their ass up and answered it.

"I don't think anyone's home. Either that or they still sleep."

"Devon, did I ask you what you think?" Devon was starting to irritate me. Like I would not have to be here banging on these people's doors looking for my girl if his ass would have tried to figure out what the hell was going on. After about five minutes, I heard some shuffling coming from the inside of the house.

"It's about fucking time," I said low under my breath. I was expecting Mr. or Mrs. Davis to answer the door. So imagine my surprise when I saw Ness' ass standing there.

"Oh, I see you got my text," he said with a smirk. "What's knockoff Chris Brown doing here?" The smirk he had on his face was now replaced with a snarl. I couldn't help but to smile. He obviously recognized Devon from the Snaps I posted on Queen's story.

"Where's Queen?" I asked, ignoring his question. I tried to push past him to get in the house, but he kept blocking my way.

"She sleep, why?"

"Why? Nigga, what do you mean why? Who the fuck do you think you are? You dragged her out my house last night." I was starting to get heated. I didn't give two fucks if he towered over me, I was ready to lay him on his ass.

"Bre chill, that's not the bul who came and got her last night," Devon said, placing his hand on my shoulder. I guess he knew I was about to pop off.

"What you mean he's not the one who got her?" I was confused as hell. If Ness wasn't the one to drag Queen out the house, who the hell was?

"Look, I don't got time for this. Give me her keys and I'll order you a uber back, my nigga," Ness promised with his hand outstretched. I just laughed. This nigga really thought I was just gonna hand her keys over and dip? He better guess again, cause I'm not going anywhere until I check on my girl.

"I'm not giving you shit! Now you can either move and let me in the house, or we can stand here all day. Shit, I ain't have nothing planned to do anyway. I got time today." I crossed my arms over my chest.

I wasn't Queen. I wasn't just gonna do what this nigga wanted me to. Shit, he had the right one today. I was with all of the shits. See Queen, bless her soul; she was too nice. Cause if I was in her shoes, this nigga would have been left in the gutta after the first fucking time he thought he was finna lay his hands on me. I swear this nigga dick game better be bomb the way she always goes back to him. It's like every time they break up, they end up fucking, and boom, it's like nothing ever happened.

I felt for her, though. She was still young and still learning the ways of the world. I just wish she never fell into the clutches of this dip shit. I never liked Ness. Queen told me the whole story of how they met. This nigga was just as bad as her uncle. She always defended him, saying he was nothing like Deon. But at the end of the day, they both like fucking on little girls. But this was Queen's life. I could give her every bit of advice I had. It was up to her to take it and put it to use. I couldn't force her, but I could protect her when and where I could, and that's what I was doing today.

Chapter 17

QUEEN

I woke up and the spot next to me was empty. I wasn't surprised though, Ness was the black Houdini. He stayed pulling a disappearing act. I reached over to my nightstand to grab my phone. That's when I remembered that I had left it at Brielle's.

"Shit," I said as I pulled back the covers. I got up and stretched. Ness really pushed my body to its limit last night. I walked over to my closet and grabbed my robe. I didn't feel like putting clothes on, plus I still needed to take a shower. As soon as I opened the door, I heard Brielle yelling.

"MY NIGGA, YOU DON'T EVEN FUCKING KNOW ME! LIKE I'M WITH THE SHITS! I DON'T NEED TO CALL NOBODY, BRO! I GOT A GLOCK, YA ASS GOING ON A T-SHIRT. SHIT, I AIN'T PAY ALL THIS MONEY FOR A PISTOL TO NOT USE IT. I DON'T GOTTA CALL NOBODY!" she was screaming, and most likely, reaching in her Louis bag that a nigga bought her just for being pretty. It was big enough for keys, phones, tampons, and her gun. This I knew for sure.

I hurried down the stairs. Whenever Bri started talking about her gun, you know she was serious.

"DEVON, LET GO OF ME!" I didn't know what was going on. All I saw was Devon was holding Bri back, and Ness was leaning against the door frame.

"Bitch, ain't nobody scared of you. You betta go head before I lay hands on you," Ness laughed.

"I'm not Queen, pussy! I'm not just gonna let you beat me like some bitch on the street."

"BRIELLE!" I screamed. I couldn't believe she would say something like that. I told her that in confidence. And she was just yelling it to the world.

Everything stopped once I yelled. Ness turned around with that stupid ass smirk on his face, like always.

"Queen, I didn't mean-" she started.

"Just save it Bri," I cut her off. "Even if you weren't, you still did." I couldn't even hold back the tears. Of all the things she could have said, it had to be that. Devon let her go, and she came running towards me. I trlied to move my legs, but they were frozen in place.

"Queen, believe me, I really didn't mean it the way it sounded." Bri pulled me into her arms. "I just...I just don't understand why you stay with someone like him," she said into the side of my face.

I was still mad as hell at her. She was right, nonetheless. Ness treated me like shit. The constant cheating and lying. Beating me like I was a dog. I deserved better. But I couldn't leave him. I wasn't ready. Every time I tried to end things, I always gave in when he came for me. I loved this man, and although I knew I deserved better, I wanted better from Ness.

"I know..." was all I could manage to get out. I wrapped my arms around Bri, and just like that our friendship was mended. Bri broke the hug and handed me my keys and my phone.

"So what the fuck happened last night? I wake up wit' ya ass gone. Devon ass don't know where you are, talking bout some old head dragged you out the house." I laughed. I could only imagine the look on Bri's face when she woke up and found me missing.

"Bitch, my ass was salty as fuck. Thinking I was about to get a homecooked breakfast and ya ass not there. I thought you got kidnapped." Bri laughed.

"Girl, this man called my dad! Me and Devon had just got out the shower when he knocked on the door."

"Oh, we taking showers with niggas now? You gave my pussy away last night?" That bit of news wiped that smirk off his face quick.

Brielle and I both turned towards Ness. I forgot his ass was standing there. I rolled my eyes. He did not want to get me started.

"Sure did. Bust her shit wide open, G." I tried to hide the smile on my face hearing Devon admitting to it. Memories from last night flooded my mind, and I couldn't stop myself from reliving the events.

"My nigga, I wasn't talking to you. Stay in a bitch place," Ness said as he started to walk towards Devon. It was too early to be dealing with all this shit. I bet my neighbors were loving act two.

"You just wanna dip?" Brielle whispered in my ear. I looked at her and nodded. I was not dealing with this shit right now. Brielle pushed Ness out the way as the two of us ran out the house to my car.

"Ay yo!" Ness laughed as we were getting in the car. I didn't even care that I was still butterball naked. I was out all night already in nothing but a towel; what was a few more hours?

Chapter 18

ANGELICA

I woke up to a bunch of screaming. I reached over to Clyde's side of his bed and found it empty. I forgot he slept in his study last night. *Oh, last night,* I thought as memories from last night's fiasco surfaced. Today was gonna be filled with nothing but pain. But I knew I owed him an explanation. I took a deep breath and got out of bed. I needed coffee topped off with some Bailey's and to figure out what the hell all the noise was. I put my slippers on and grabbed my housecoat. Making my way down the stairs, I saw my door was wide open.

"Now, who the hell-" Before I could finish the sentence, there was Ness, face to face with some light skinned boy, and Queen was pulling off in her car with someone who looked to be Brielle. So last night's drama followed into the morning. I just closed and locked my door. One of the neighbors was bound to call the cops eventually. So my hands would be washed of whatever the hell was going on outside. I walked to the kitchen and started to brew my coffee and make breakfast for Clyde and I. I didn't know how I was gonna face that man. This was all shit. I didn't want to have the conversation without Queen being present. Hopefully, he would just ignore me for the time being. I was gonna leave Queen alone for now too. We all needed a break from each other.

I decided I was gonna try to get back in Clyde's favor. Even though I knew no matter what I did, it wouldn't make him forget my betrayal. I was fixing his favorite breakfast. Steak, scrambled eggs with cheese, and cheesy grits. Was this gonna be enough? No. What it was, was a step in the right direction. Clyde only got this breakfast on holidays or his birthday. He knew if I was serving this to him on a normal day, it symbolized an apology and me waving the white flag. I knew keeping it to myself wasn't the right thing to do. But how was I to bring that to my husband when I myself did not know who to believe? I did what I thought was best at the time. Maybe I was wrong.

Not too long after I was done cooking, my husband walked into the kitchen. I stayed silent, knowing he wouldn't have returned any greeting I gave him. I served him his food and sat down to eat myself.

"We have to talk about this," he began.

I really didn't want to have this conversation right now. I just sat silently and sipped my coffee. "I'm very upset, Angelica. That's not even the word. I don't know what the damn word is for what I am. How could you keep something like this away from me? Your brother has been touching our daughter. Your child. The child you carried for nine months. How could you not say anything to me?"

At this point, tears were rolling from my eyes. Clyde was much calmer than I'd assume he'd be. I couldn't bring myself to even look at him. Deon was my older brother. He practically raised me. Our parents were around but not really involved with us. Deon, though, always made sure I was straight. That's the only reason why he was in the streets. He made sure we always had money to get what we needed or what we wanted. Our parents were selfish. They never wanted us, so they did the bare minimum. Making sure we had food. That was it. They didn't care if we had clothes for school, or if we were properly taking care of. Deon wasn't just my brother; he was my father in a sense. I should have known something like this was gonna happen.

I should have just told Clyde. I should have believed Queen. Cause Deon used to touch me as well. I never told anyone about it. Deon told me I owed it to him for taking care of me. I didn't think anything of it then because I didn't know any better.

As I grew older, I knew what he was doing to me was wrong. I continued to keep it to myself because by then, I was ashamed, felt it was my fault, and felt like I owed him for everything he's ever done for me. So, I kept our little secret. Even Clyde didn't know. I imagine if he did, he would have never let him in the house and around our child. I thought after me he wouldn't do something like this anymore. Yet I was wrong, and after years of suffering alone. I had to break the silence for my daughter's sake.

"Angelica, you hear me talking to you?" Clyde's voice grew louder. He was growing tired of the silence I was responding with. I couldn't bring myself to answer him though. I wanted him, and Queen to both hear my story at the same time. If I had to talk about it, it was only gonna be once. I didn't want to relive the hurt I had buried so deep in my past.

"I... I want to wait 'til Queen is here. There's something you both need to hear," I managed to say. It was barely a whisper.

"But why didn't you tell me?" Clyde asked again, making his voice soft. I fell silent once again. I was not gonna answer until both were present. I was standing on that. Clyde stood up and just walked away. I didn't realize I was holding my breath until I let it out. I just prayed they didn't think I was playing the victim.

Chapter 19

DEON

I t was a normal day for me. I was just getting back to the house from collecting some money that was owed to me. These young niggas nowadays thought they could slick a can of oil. Like I was a fool or something. I could tell when they were short just by holding the stack they would give me. No need to count it. I was just about to kick my shoes off when I got a text from Clyde. Apparently, he and Angelica wanted to speak with me. I didn't have time for this. All I wanted to do was chill for the rest of the day. What could they possibly want to talk to me about? I replied back and headed to the kitchen. I wasn't gonna go there hungry. Besides, I didn't know what I was about to walk into. I damn sure wasn't going to be going on an empty stomach.

I made myself two sandwiches and went to my basement. It's where I kept my private collection of home movies. I settled down in the La-Z-Boy I had down there and turned on the tape that was already in the VCR. It was me and my little Queen. She had to be about nine then. I watched the tape and compared her to how she was now. If only I could get to her now that she's fully developed. I know she's my niece but damn. She had a body like her mama did back then. Shit, from time to time, I still got some of Ange, but after she got married, I chilled out on that. Then she gave birth to Queen. It was like having Ange all over again.

I didn't even finish my first sandwich before I got turned on and needed to relieve myself. After I busted my nut, I cleaned up and headed upstairs to take a shower. I had to get Queen alone again. I needed to experience that new body of hers. She was too old to need me to babysit for her, so I have to think of another way to be alone with her. Which was hard since she had that little boyfriend or whatever. I can't even call that nigga little. He was a grown ass man. Had to be at least eight years older than her; at least I thought so. Still don't know what Clyde was thinking when he found out about him. How he was ok with Queen being with him. I could never forgive him for that.

Chapter 20

QUEEN

Brielle and I had to stop at her house so I could put some clothes on. I had come to my senses and was not finna be driving around in a bathrobe all day. On the way to her house, I had to catch her up on all the events of last night. I swear I felt like I was trapped in a Lifetime movie. This is some shit those white folks be going through. You never hear about no black people going through shit like this.

"Are you serious? Girl, that couldn't be me. I can't believe your dad did that to you," Brielle said.

"Bitch, not only did he drag me out your house while Devon was standing there, when we pulled up to the house, Ness' ass was standing there." We had just pulled up to Bri's house and sat in the car for a bit to finish the conversation.

"Speaking of his ass, why the hell was he still there this morning?" I rolled my eyes. I didn't want to talk about this. I knew Bri was just worried about me. I just didn't want to hear what she always said.

"Bri, you know why he was there. And please don't lecture me. I already know what you're going to say. You're right. I'm just not

ready to move on from him yet." With that, I took my key out of the
ignition and got out of the car. I didn't want to keep hearing how I
deserved better or needed to find someone new. It was getting
exhausting. I knew I did, but I wanted Ness.

We got in the house, and I immediately went straight to her
bathroom to wash myself up. I loved being at Bri's house. It was my
home away from home. I had a good amount of my stuff here. I
never had to bring anything along with me when I came over to visit.
I checked my phone while I turned on the shower and waited for the
shower to heat up. I had a few missed calls from Ness and like three
texts. I was gonna deal with that later. Too much has happened in the
last couple hours. I just wanted to relax before returning to the shit
show. I put on *Bang* by Jessie J, Ariana Grande, and Nicki Minaj. I
was jamming while I washed away the stress from last night.

After my shower, I went to Bri's guest room and got dressed. I
kept all my good clothes over here. Cause my dad would drawl about
most of the shit I wear. I grabbed my white crop top, my light blue
skinny jeans, and my white Air Force One's. I was looking badd as
hell. I put my hair in a messy bun, swooped my edges and applied
some clear lip gloss. Yea I was looking damn fine. I took a picture for
Snap, went downstairs and waited for Bri to finish getting ready.

Thirty minutes later, Bri and I were sitting in the nail salon. This
is what I needed. Time to relax. There was too much shit on my
mind.

"I still can't believe Devon just let you get dragged out the house.
Like whoo the fucks does that?"

"Girl, I was sitting in my dad's car thinking about that shit. Like
what if I was really getting kidnapped and that nigga just let it
happen." I laughed. We talked about Devon for a little while more
before Bri changed the subject.

"I was waiting to tell you this under better circumstances,"

Brielle began. "I'm gonna be moving soon. I need a change of scenery." I couldn't believe it. The only person I could confide in was leaving me. As if I didn't already have enough to deal with.

"When and where?" I asked, looking straight ahead. I was gonna miss having Bri around, but her moving didn't mean we weren't gonna be able to see each other.

"I found this cute two bedroom in Harrisburg. I'm going to sign the lease next week. And then I move in two weeks later." I nodded my head. I didn't know what to say. I was happy for her, obviously, but I wanted her here with me.

"Queen, don't make that face. You know my door is always open for you. Why you think I got a two bedroom?" Brielle said. "You're eighteen now. So whenever you're ready to get out of your parent's house, your room will be ready." I smiled at her. Though it was bitter sweet, I knew Brielle was always gonna be there for me.

After we were done getting our nails done, we grabbed something to eat and did some much needed retail therapy. We stayed at the mall 'til they closed. During that time, I had so many missed calls from my mom, dad and Ness. Devon never hit me up, which I wasn't worried about. I didn't think it was gonna progress between us anyway. He was just a nice fuck and, obviously, a punk. I dropped Bri off back home.

Before I pulled away, I took a deep breath. Since I was ignoring everyone's call, I didn't know what was waiting for me back at home. I drove home in silence. I wanted to get my thoughts together and try to prepare for what I thought was waiting for me. But I would never be ready for what I walked into.

I pulled into the driveway and the first thing I noticed was Deon's car. *What the hell is he doing here?* I thought as I got out of the car. I hurried to make my way to the front door. I unlocked it and walked into the house.

"Mom!?" I screamed so I could figure out what room she was in.

"We're in the living room, Queen." I heard my mom say. I made my way to the living room. My mom, dad, and uncle Deon were all sitting there.

"Why haven't you been answering your phone?" My dad asked, standing up.

"I must have had the ringer on silent. I haven't checked my phone all day," I lied. I couldn't tell my dad I was intentionally ignoring their calls. It would have started a whole argument.

"Well, from now on, make sure your ringer is on." My dad sat back down. I couldn't tell if he believed me or not, but I wasn't going to press the issue.

"What's going on? Why is...Why is uncle Deon here?" I asked, looking at my mom for answers.

"Queen, don't act like that. Come give me some love. Is it wrong for me to come see my favorite niece?" Deon stood up and stepped towards me, and I backed away.

"Deon, you may want to sit back down. I'm not gonna be able to hold myself accountable if you touch my daughter," my dad said in a low voice.

"What the hell is that supposed to mean?" Deon asked, looking over at him with a grin on his face.

"Deon, just sit the fuck down! Queen, sit over there." My dad pointed to the single seat chair across from him and my mom. I did as I was told. I didn't know what was going on. But if I had to guess, it had to be what went down last night.

"You acting real funny, Clyde. I can't even give my own niece a hug? Ange, what the fuck is his problem?" The room was filled with tension and no one was talking. My mom and dad were looking at the floor. Deon was looking at my mom for answers. I just sat there trying to figure out what everyone else was thinking.

"I wanted to wait to have this conversation, because I wanted Queen to be here for this. Now that she is, I'm not sure of where to start," my mother began. She took a deep breath and looked up at me.

"Queen, the reason you never see my parents is rather simple. They never wanted me; they never wanted your uncle Deon either. Deon raised me. He took care of me. Did everything our parents were supposed to do. I couldn't ask for a better older brother." Deon smiled and nodded, no doubt giving himself props for what my mother was saying.

"Get to the point, Angelica.," my father said. I noticed a hint of irritation in his voice as he spoke.

"Not only did Deon raise me, he also sexually abused me for years," she finally got out, looking like it hurt to even say.

"Angelica, that's some bullshit! Don't sit there and lie to that girl. I sexually assaulted you, really? That's how you feel?" Uncle Deon was standing up at this point.

"Deon, I'm not gonna tell you again, sit your ass the fuck down!" My father screamed. I never heard my dad use the F word before.

"Mom, what are you-" I began, shocked at what was being said there in that moment.

"Queen, let her finish. I wanna hear this," my dad said, cutting me off.

"I'm a grown ass man, Clyde. I'm not your fucking child. I don't know why Ange sitting here lying to y'all like this, but I'm not gonna stay around and be accused of something I didn't do." Deon started walking towards the door. My dad got up so quick you would have thought he was The Flash. I screamed when I saw he had a gun pointed at Deon's head.

"I'm gonna say it one more time, sit your ass down." Deon didn't even flinch. It obviously wasn't the first time he's been in a situation like this, I assume. If so, wouldn't he have some type of reaction?

"Dad, what are you-"

"Queen, shut up." My dad slowly started to back away but still had the gun pointed at Deon. He didn't sit down until Deon was back on the couch.

"Since Angelica is taking her sweet time, I'm going to be doing the talking. Deon, you're creating one hell of a mess for my family. It recently came to my attention that you've been touching my daughter here. And now I'm learning you also touched my wife. What would you do if you were me?" My dad asked.

"Man, I ain't never touched either one of them." Deon was sticking to this story of his. Even with a gun pointed straight at him, he wasn't afraid to lie.

"That's funny. You think I didn't notice how Queen backed away from you when you tried to hug her moments ago? To my knowledge, Queen only ever had one boyfriend. If I tell her to call him and tell him to come over, do you think he'd tell me she was a virgin the first time they ever had sex?"

This was beginning to make me extremely uncomfortable. I did not want to sit here and have my sex life discussed in front of my family. By now, I was crying. It was all becoming too much for me to handle. I wished I never would have brought any of this up last night. I wished I never even told my mom. If I hadn't, none of this would be happening right now.

Deon looked over at me, his face hard as stone. I couldn't tell what he was thinking. I didn't like how he was looking at me. It reminded me of how he would look at me when I was younger.

"Queen, baby, would you please inform your father that I never touched you?" he had the fucking nerve to say.

Was he really asking me to protect him right now? Why did he even think I would lie for him? He and I both know what he did, and he wanted me to lie for him. Not today. Today was his day to get what he deserved. It was the day for the truth to come out. It must have been hard as hell for my mom to admit what she had just let out. Looking at her, she was just staring straight ahead, eyes glassy, as if in shock. I knew she couldn't have been lying and if she was letting it out after all this time, so was my ass.

"Yes you did," I said in a low voice, looking down at the floor.

"Queen, speak up. You know I hate it when you mumble," my

dad responded. I took a deep breath. I could taste the saltiness of my tears as I did so. I was crying so much that when I opened my mouth, they slid right in.

"Deon... uncle Deon, has been touching me for a long while. I never said anything because I was afraid you and mom wouldn't believe me. When I finally told mom, she told me, she said... not to mention it and that he would never do something like that because he loved me like his own daughter. It's when I knew he was right all these years. No one would believe me if my own mother didn't. That's when I started to shut down and really rebel," I let it all out. Everything I had been holding back.

"So, Angelica, it was your idea to keep this from me. Knowing that he touched you, or so you claim, you still allowed this man to be alone with our daughter?" he questioned with disgust in his voice and eyes.

"I... I didn't think he would touch her, Clyde. I...I ... I thought it ended with me."

The room fell silent once again. It was an eerie silence, everyone was lost in their own thoughts. I was hoping and praying dad wasn't gonna shoot Deon right here in our living room. I just wanted this all to be over. Wishing that it was just a bad dream.

"Do you have anything to say for yourself, Deon? Cause honestly, I believe you did it," my father said, cocking the gun.

"Like I said before, I didn't touch either one of them," he continued. A lying ass coward 'til the end.

"Well, for the sake of everyone here, please stay away from my family. It would be a sad state of affairs if something were to happen to you," my dad let him know, standing up with the gun still pointed at him. "Now, get the hell out of my house. And don't show your face around here again." With that being said, Deon got up to leave.

My dad, who was walking behind him with the gun still pointed, hit him in the back with the gun. He fell right as his hand touched the door. My mother yelled out. He then kicked him in the face while he was down there. I stood up and ran towards my father, thinking he would shoot Deon. Not that he didn't earn a bullet between the eyes, but the last thing I wanted was my daddy in prison for murder. Even if he was happy to go for me. My mom grabbed my arms and pushed my face into her chest, trying to stop me from seeing what may happen next. Her face buried in my head and her tears, mixing with mine as they fell.

"Ahhh, what the fuck, Clyde?!" he said, trying to get up.

"That's just a reminder of what would be waiting for you if I hear you have tried to contact either one of my girls again. I know your big shit in the street, but to me, you're a fucking filthy pedophile. So, promise me your ass will stay away from my family, or you can die, slow, or go to prison with the tag of a child rapist. That would turn out real good for you in there, I hear," he went on calmly, still pointing the gun at him as he was down on the floor.

"I promise..." My uncle managed to get out as I could hear him scramble to his feet, and then the door shut behind him.

Not hearing the gunshot I thought I would, I wedged myself away from my mom's embrace and ran to my daddy. He looked at me, tears in his eyes, and then took me my head and brought me into him, letting me cry until there were no tears left.

One month later...

I was sitting on the couch watching the news and on the phone with Ness. Life had somewhat gotten back to normal at home, but there were still a few eggshells we were walking on. Brielle moved to Harrisburg like she planned. I went up there once to help her move. I hadn't really been able to leave the house unless it was for work or I was with Ness. One of the many rules my dad had put into place. He wanted to know everything I was doing at all times. Mom and I's relationship was still strained.

After I learned about Deon touching her and then she turned around and didn't even believe me when I came to her about him touching me, I couldn't stand to be around her most of the time. I feel like she tried to make me seem as if I were a liar or crazy when she knew what he was capable of the whole time. She's been trying her hardest to try to make it up to me, but nothing she did would ever make me forgive her.

"So, you're still picking me up on Friday, right? I can't be in this house any longer," I directed towards Ness. I knew He was still out in New York trying to be sneaky. If he could have his cake and eat it too, why couldn't I? Little did he know I would tell my dad I had to work late some nights, but I was really out getting my back broke. If this was the game he wanted to play, we could do that. I wasn't going to be the only one in this relationship looking stupid.

"Yea, I'm still coming to get you. You already know I need some of that sweet pussy. Nigga over here going through a drought." I rolled my eyes cause I knew his ass was lying.

"Breaking news, Police officers found Deon Smith shot dead in his home after a neighbor called to report hearing multiple gunshots. Police reported that Deon suffered from five shots, four to the chest and one to the head."

I couldn't believe what I was hearing. Deon was dead! I looked around to see if anyone else was hearing this. I was in a state of shock, I also caught a smile spreading across my face. If he hadn't raped me, I would have felt bad. But I was smiling from ear to ear.

"Babe, I'm gonna call you back later. I gotta deal with something real quick," I said into the phone.

"Ard cool. I gotta go run some errands anyway. Love you."

"Love you too." Just as we hung up the phone, I heard the front door open. I turned to see who it was and it was my dad. He looked at the T.V and then back at me with a knowing look in his eye. We never spoke on it. This was a secret worth keeping, for once. I knew he was responsible for Deon's murder. I realized in that moment that he loved me the best he could. Even though Deon's death proved that, it didn't fix the broken people he left behind. That was the real tragedy.

Present Day

"Wait, you telling me your dad killed your uncle?" Logan asked in shock.

"I'm not telling you anything. I never found out for sure. But I do have a hunch he was responsible for his death," I said as I sipped on my wine. We were sitting in the living room just enjoying each other's company when he asked to know the history between me and Ness. I guess he was still trying to process why I reacted the way I did when he was killed. Ness was a no good piece of shit who gaslit me every chance he had. But the love I had for that man was real. So it was only natural I did feel some type of way about him dying. However, I did not attend the funeral.

"So what happened with that Brook girl? I know you had to deal with her ass again," Logan said, trying to juice every detail he could from out of me. We are married now. I guess he wanted to know a little bit more about my life story and how I became the person sitting before him.

"Babe, I found out this bitch was stalking my Facebook. Since you know Brielle and I are petty with a capital P, I started stealing her photos and posting her as my woman crush Monday." I laughed at the memory. This bitch would get so mad and have Ness calling me to take her photos down.

"For real? Y'all crazy. Remind me not to do nun stupid then. I could only imagine what y'all asses would do to me." He tried to joke.

"Oh, Brielle was gonna kill you," I said, drinking more of my wine.

"What you mean she was gonna kill me?" He asked, shocked, taking my glass from me.

"Remember when I went to the spot and that dumb bitch was there trying to say you sent her and showed me a picture of the two of you on our couch? Yeah, Brielle was ready to beat ya head in with a bat. Lucky for you, I stopped her," I said so casually, like it was so long ago when all that drama with Isidora happened.

Truth be told, it wasn't. It was still fresh in all of our minds. Logan had PTSD so bad he would stay up all night in Elara's room watching her sleep. I couldn't have him making himself sick from not sleeping, so for the time being, all three of us slept in the master bedroom together. It was gonna be a long time before we could get back to acting normally.

"Can I have my wine back, Please?" I asked, annoyed.

"Nope. I don't give a fuck what Google tell you. You lucky I even let you have a couple sips, but you not drinking a whole glass of wine while my son in there," he said, putting the wine glass out of my reach. "You got two more months, babe; hang in there." He leaned in to kiss me because he knew damn well my fat ass was not moving unless it was necessary.

At least our lives were finally getting back to normal somewhat. And now that both of our demons had been exercised, we could give our daughter, and little Logan; when he got here, what we didn't have and always wanted, a safe, drama-free life. Well, we were gonna damn well try...

AVAILABLE ON AMAZON

AVAILABLE ON AMAZON

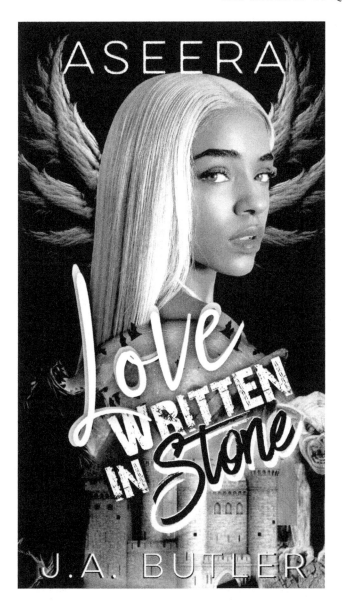

COMING SOON